Partly Sunny

An Honest and Humorous Look at the
First Weeks of Bringing Home a Newborn

WHITNEY BAUSMAN

DEDICATION

To Jonathan, who gave me my two most precious gifts,
and to Clark and Annie, who made me Mom.

CONTENTS

ACKNOWLEDGMENTS

Jonathan, you are my rock and my encourager. This book wouldn't have been possible without your belief in me, your support, and your "go for it!" spirit that I love so very much. Thank you.

Sue, not only were you my editor and my sounding board for this project, but you are my friend and someone who I am genuinely grateful to live life with. Thank you.

Mom, Alicia, and Ashley, you are my heroes, and you made this collection of memories come to life by helping me piece together the mess. You make me laugh, you put me back together when I fall apart, and you make me strive to be a better mother and human being every day.

Kelly, you are my best friend, and your encouragement means more to me than you will ever know. I hope and pray that this book has helped you in some small way for the journey ahead. I can't wait to meet your little boy in a few, short weeks.

Stacy, you are my sanity preserver. Thank you for your candor and your vulnerability. When you revealed your just-like-me frustrations in those first days of mommyhood, it was then that life was breathed into this work.

Carey, thank you for your perfectly timed "gift".

To all of those who read a raw version of my work or who boosted my spirit when I wanted to let these words grow dusty—Dad Bausman, Mom Bausman, Tara, Doreen, Kristina, and countless others—thank you.

PREFACE: CAUTION TAPE

If you're reading this book, chances are you are either A: a pregnant first-timer looking for a little insight on the journey ahead, B: a parent in the thick of raising (and surviving!) children, yearning for comedic relief from someone who *feels you*, or C: a family member or friend of mine wanting to see what my thoughts look like when they make it to paper. Whoever you are, welcome! This book is for you.

To those in Group A... congratulations! Have you taken a moment today to bask in the crazy-amazing thing your body is doing? Think about it. Totally nuts, right?! Nuts-in-a-good-way, awe-inspiring, and wonderful, yes... but let's keep it real, guys, hard *work* too. If you haven't figured it out already, being pregnant, at least for the vast majority of womenfolk, isn't always a cup of tea. As I said to an expecting friend of mine just yesterday, pregnancy is a weird and hard time. You're literally growing a mini-person inside of you, and your own body is "growing" too, contrary to the desires of basically every woman ever. It's a rollercoaster ride of hormones, exhaustion, sickness, and the often unwelcome advice of any and all whose eyes lay sight on your growing bump. This book is for you. (Pregnancy partner? Believe me, it's for *you* too. You're going to need what follows just as much as she does when life gets really crazy, really soon...)

To those in Group B... how'd you (not) sleep last night? Maybe you're new to this whole gig of parenthood and have a tiny infant who demands seeing your face, or boobs, several times a night. Maybe you're further down the pike and have a toddler or two who somehow always find their way into

1

(what used to be) *your* bed. Maybe you've got a few more years under your belt and had a super-fun, sleepless night cleaning vomit from your school-aged child's hair, and pajamas, and sheets, and floor, and walls. Even more seasoned, you say? Maybe *you* spent the night awake helping your teenager put the final touches on his or her could-this-get-any-more-complicated Science Fair project. Wherever you are, parents, this book is for you.

To those in Group C… I think I pity you all the most. You're the folks who actually know me and have a pretty good chance of seeing my face again after reading the contents of the following pages. I'm really sorry. I'm especially giggly when I think about my father-in-law, who has been so supportive of this project, reading page after page of my tell-all tales of lady parts. This is going to be hilarious (for me). Just remember that you were warned.

On the topic of warnings, I feel the need to take some space for several caveats before we dig deep and get started:

- Haters Gonna Hate

T Swift[1] got it right on this one. In the chapters to come, I am going to say very candid, very real, and, at times, very ugly things. There are certainly going to be folks out there who don't support my openness and altogether lack of couth. Some may even question my ability to be a good mother. Quite frankly, I'm okay with that. I *intensely* love my children and would do anything to keep them safe, healthy, and feeling nurtured. That doesn't mean I have to have loved every minute of pregnancy, childbirth, and/or the messy aftermath. I know my heart, and God knows my heart, and that's good enough for me.

- Rainbows and Butterflies

The overarching theme of this collection of thoughts and memories is the stark difference between my *expectations* of motherhood and the *realities* of my transition from melon-carrier to Mom. Thanks to greeting cards, children's literature, and the well-meaning expressions of loved ones, I always pictured the first weeks of a baby's life being filled with rainbows and butterflies for infant and parents alike. What I actually experienced, however, was partly sunny with an occasional caterpillar spotting. Again, guys, I l o v e d and adored each of my babes from the get-go, but exhaustion, discomfort, doubt, and guilt are *normal* realities of bringing a child into the world. Realities that we aren't talking about enough. If you're a mom or dad reading this who truly had a picture-perfect (or even a close to perfect) experience, you deserve an honest-to-goodness "Good for you!". I actually have a friend who I would put into this category. Sometimes (or so I've been told, at least…haha), babies have very easygoing, content, and calm temperaments, and sometimes, these babies are gifted to similarly-minded, chill, resilient parents. In this case, sure, perhaps there are rainbows. Let me be bold, however, and say that this is not the norm. It's just not. Take a stab at guessing whose babies weren't easygoing and who was anything-but-chill as a new mom. Yep. That would be me.

- Scare Tactics

Please know that my intentions are never to scare any of you, especially the pregnant readers out there and their brave, often-antagonized-by-hunger-and-hormones partners. If, by the end of this book, your legs are inadvertently crossed tighter than they ever have been before and you are praying that your bundle just decides to stay put indefinitely, I have done you a disservice. What I hope you find in reading these pages, instead, is humor in the midst of what can be a very overwhelming, tiring, and isolating experience. I want you to be able to laugh with me now so that you won't feel crazy later if and when the same things happen to you.

- Keeping it Real

If I've learned one thing since becoming a parent, it's that things can be terrible and wonderful at the same time. Things can be weird, and gross, and exhausting, and hard, but still be hilarious, and beautiful, and the best-ever. My kids are who I am. I love them with a ferocity that I never even knew I possessed prior to parenthood. There's so much good in what they've brought to my life and that of my amazing, supportive husband. The goodness is only half of the picture, however, and if my goal is transparency (which it surely is), I simply have to keep it real and be true to myself so that I can be true to you.

- Weltschmerz (pronounced 'velt-shmerts) is No Joke

Why get real and publicize so many private, raw moments? Because these things are normal, they're important, and they're the things that no one ever tells you. About two years ago, I was blessed to share in the experience of pregnancy with my good friend, Stacy. I was due with baby number two only a few weeks before Stacy was due with baby number one. Because of this, I offered her encouragement and support as she needed it, especially when she told me that this was the first baby to be born on either side of her and her husband's family. Months down the road, my sweetie arrived and Stacy's due date approached. I kept feeling a strong pull to get real with my friend and send her a quick email so that she'd know it was totally okay for her not to have a picturesque experience. My "quick" email turned out to be pages long, and as I prepared to hit 'send', I was overwhelmingly nervous about how my words would be received. Would I scare her, or do more harm than good? Would I make myself look like a horrible mother? I swallowed my fears, clicked the button, and then sweat postpartum, hormonal bullets until I heard something (ANYTHING!) in response. What I received, at first, was a true-to-Stacy reply, something along the lines of:

- "Thank you for being honest with me. I so appreciate it and will be sure to take all of these things to heart when baby arrives."

This is what I expected from my sweet, proper friend who always sees the best in everything. What I *didn't* expect were the messages I received *after* baby arrived. Messages that looked and sounded a whole lot more like me. Messages that wholeheartedly thanked me for helping a new mom not to feel awful, alone, and completely disheartened when realities and expectations failed to align. This is Weltschmerz, a term I happened upon when researching for the work you hold in your hands. Weltschmerz is "mental depression or apathy caused by comparison of the actual state of the world with an ideal state"[2]. Yesssssssss. Weltschmerz was my experience, and Stacy's, and I'm guessing a whole lot of other parents' when their little ones made it to town. Would the world be a little less Weltschmerz-y if we had more realistic expectations of becoming a mom or dad? Perhaps. For this reason, I made it a mission to take my thoughts and feelings to the masses. End result? You're reading it.

- What I am Not, and Not

First things first, I am not a doctor. I may be a nurse, by trade, but I am in no way, shape, or form trying to provide medical advice in the confines of these pages. While I may share recollections and experiences that depict a time in my life that wasn't as sunny as I'd hoped it would be, I have never experienced postpartum depression nor do I have the ability to speak to overcoming that obstacle. Please, if in becoming a mother you ever feel depressed beyond hope, lack a connection with your baby, or consider harming anyone in any way, get in touch with your medical provider *immediately*. You are not alone.

Second things second, I am not able to speak from personal experience regarding miscarriage, high-risk pregnancy, high-risk delivery, and/or infant loss. While some of my closest loved ones have found themselves in these very dark, debilitating circumstances, I am one of the lucky few who has only ever experienced "typical", predictable, by-the-books pregnancies and non-surgical deliveries. If you have already been to one of these places and back and are choosing to read this book, I am so very humbled for you to join me. From the most serious place of respect and sympathy, I am sorry that you have been where you have been. I can see how many of my *negative* sentiments regarding childbirth and the newborn days could be painful and difficult for you to swallow when you would have given anything to have my experience. What I have learned in recent years, however, is that my reality isn't changed or minimized because of someone else's... it is simply placed into perspective. So while I may have had my share of ugly in the days following the births of both of my children, I must be reminded that my ugly could have been a whole lot uglier. Even if our journeys look vastly different, I sincerely hope that we can laugh together from this point forward.

All of this being said, welcome aboard the bare-it-all, share-it-all voyage that was and is my life. What you're about to read won't be pretty and lined with gold, but it will be true, and honest, and authentic. Whoever you are, and wherever you are, I pray that this book gives you laughter, some insight, a dose of reality, and a whole lot of hope (my favorite word in the entire English language). If I can help *one* soul out there to feel a little less alone or crazy on this adventure we call parenthood, then I have done what I seek to do through these pages.

---

1. Taylor Swift. "Shake it Off." *1989*, Big Machine, 2014.
2. "Weltschmerz." Def.1. *Merriam-Webster.com*. Merriam-Webster. Web. 1 Dec. 2017.

1   THINGS YOU SHOULDN'T THINK OR SAY

My firstborn arrived just after 9:30 PM in a birthing suite directly next to a family waiting room. Throughout the process of delivery, this waiting room housed my mom, my mother-in-law, my father-in-law, my aunt, and my two sisters. After the baby and I were medically cleared and settled, my husband, Jonathan, ventured next door to inform our (beyond) excited and eager family members that we had welcomed a son into the world, whom we named Clark. I didn't have to guess when that announcement was made as the collective screams of my loved ones lit up the entire labor and delivery hall. My family members were literally "shushed" like a bunch of naughty kindergarteners, which is so fitting and cracks me up to this day. Add to our clan my brother-in-law and sister-in-law who trekked over from the postpartum floor (they had delivered their firstborn just a day before), and we had quite a little welcoming party for our guy. The first few hours of Clark's life were filled with the smiles and happy tears of not only Jonathan and I, but many of those we love most in this life.

Looking back on it now, I was so full of hormones and hype in those "first moments." Although I was a bit of a sweaty, shaky mess thanks to adrenaline, I was in awe of what my body had just done. I was holding a perfect little boy in my arms. I had a son. I was a mom. My hubby beamed with pride and was adorably reduced to tears every five seconds, and I had never loved or appreciated him more. We were surrounded by our closest supporters, none of which could wipe the smiles from their faces. Truly, everything just felt right in the world. These beautiful, much-welcomed, and *expected* "first moments" are some of the most special and sacred of my 31 years. The moments that followed them, however? The unfiltered and *unexpected* "second moments" that caught me by surprise… moments that weren't smile-filled or consumed by happy thoughts? Well, they were difficult to swallow.

I'm convinced that when it comes to having a newborn, there are two distinct lines of thinking. First, there are the things you *think* you'll think prior to parenthood and, then, there are the things you *actually* think upon becoming a parent. The differences between the two? Significant, noteworthy and, for me anyway, just plain huge. The things you *think* you'll think are happy things, and nice things, and things similar to all of the bits of wisdom and encouragement I'm sure you heard (or will hear) time and time again throughout pregnancy. These are the "babies are such blessings" and "being a parent is the best job" sorts of things. What you may actually think, though? I'm here to tell you that it might be a whole lot less presentable—or in today's terms, Facebook-ready.

What if I told you that within mere hours of becoming a mother, I questioned whether or not I had made the biggest mistake of my life? What if I told you that despite loving my child deeply, there were moments early on when I didn't love being a parent at all? What if I told you that instead of including the adjectives I had anticipated, like "wonderful", "amazing", "beautiful", or "perfect", many of my first thoughts as a new mom contained descriptors more like "awful"? My thoughts? My real-life, new parent thoughts? Here are a few of them in their honest, terrible glory.

- "This is the worst."
- "Why exactly do people do this?"
- "<u>Never</u> happening again."

Oh, and just wait, here's the clincher:

- "Maybe we shouldn't have done this."

Eww, right? Who even thinks, let alone admits to thinking, these sorts of things as a new mom? What sort of parent goes so quickly from pristine "first moments" to mucky "second moments"? What kind of a person must I be, or have been, in order to be able to hold my own child and still have such ugly thoughts? The answer to these questions is a person who simply thought that parenthood was going to look and feel a lot different than it actually did in the beginning. When the images of my pre-parent hopes didn't quite line up with the realities of my actual-parent existence… I found myself in a place with lots of thoughts that new moms just don't go around parading.

When the sleepless nights felt long and endless? When my baby wailed despite my best efforts to figure out what he needed? When breastfeeding was cumbersome and complicated and uncomfortable and looked so far from the images in my head or the pamphlets I'd been given? When I simultaneously wanted company yet felt overwhelmed by the presence of visitors? When I found myself in unexplainable tears? When I looked at my husband and wondered if he and I would have a moment to ourselves ever again? Yeah. These were the times when less-than-pretty thoughts prevailed and parenthood just wasn't the "blessing" I was promised. Despite the well-wishers of my pregnancy days who had willed for me (over and over and over again) that I "enjoy every moment," I just didn't. I wasn't even close.

So why, then, was there such a mix-up between the expectations and realities of life as a new parent for me? Well, I think it's twofold. For starters, the nature of the experience itself (on the surface, anyway) is a beautiful thing, which led me to have beautiful hopes. If you strip away the sweat and pain of labor and delivery, childbirth really is an exhilarating, miraculous experience. Ask just about any parent out there to list for you the five very best days of their life, and I can almost promise you that the birthday(s) of their child(ren) will be included. What's more, if you strip away the sleep deprivation and the demands of caring for a newborn, becoming a parent is pretty awesome. Transitioning from a couple to a family is—plain and simple—a cool thing to witness or be a part of. And newborns? I mean, come on guys, there is nothing on Earth better than holding a tiny, sleeping baby on your chest. Babies are just cute, and squishy, and capable of turning even the most burly of men into a puddle of mush. Babies bring lots of good things into a world that doesn't often look good at all anymore, and that's kind of a big deal.

On top of the beautiful nature of the childbirth experience, as a whole, there's lots of beautiful *talk* that often leads expecting parents down a road of false expectations. Positive, cutesy, and cliché things are strewn upon soon-to-be parents by the boatload. It's no surprise, really, that the well-meaning folks in our lives bombard us with happy, sappy comments during pregnancy. As we've already established, becoming a parent is "pretty" from a surface-level perspective, and it's only natural for others to share the good bits of welcoming a newborn into the world because it's human nature to emphasize the positive and minimize the negative. We highlight all the good stuff—the cute onesies, perfect shades of pink and blue with which to paint nurseries, and trendy-cool baby names—while sweeping the not-so-good stuff under the rug for naive and unsuspecting new parents to discover for themselves. For those of us who have experienced parenthood firsthand, we don't want to scare our loved ones away from joining us on the ride. Totally wrecked post-delivery bodies, hormonal breakdowns, and even marital tension fueled by sleep deprivation? These things aren't exactly sweet and bubbly conversation points to broach with new and soon-to-be parents, but guess what? Real life.

If you're a pregnant reader who is in the midst of the flurry of advice, wisdom, and encouragement, I'm willing to bet that the majority of the things you hear are warm and fuzzy. I'm also willing to bet that when you do hear something that isn't 100% warm and fuzzy, it most often relates to the subject of sleeping… or *not* sleeping, to be more accurate. We all know that the gift of a full night's sleep is most likely a several-month, if not several-year, sacrifice on the part of one or both parents when a baby arrives on the scene. Because of this, opening up about the sleep you certainly won't be getting as a new parent is sort of a "safe spot" when it comes to people being just-a-tad honest with expecting moms and dads.

Sleep deprivation is definitely real, to the point that I'll spend an entire chapter discussing the realities of exhaustion soon enough. The reality, however, is that the woes of new parenthood stretch far beyond sleep deprivation. While I wholeheartedly believe that fatigue is at the core of the struggle and makes every aspect of caring for a newborn harder, there are lots of other hard things I didn't expect as a new mom simply because no one ever told me to. Namely, it was hard to come to terms with the basic fact that I didn't love the process of becoming a parent.

I didn't love the physical, emotional, and hormonal mess I had turned into. The fact that I was swollen and sore almost literally from head to toe, too? Not super fun or flattering. Then, there were the demands of my new, 24/7 job to consider. Seeing 2AM, and 3AM, and 4AM, and basically every other hour of the entire day for reasons beyond my control just wasn't something I enjoyed. Who would? What's more, I didn't love the way I felt because of the awful things I was thinking. The things I *didn't think* I'd think.

When my thoughts were plenty gross-sounding and had me finding fault in something that I thought was supposed to be picture-perfect apart from being tired, I felt like the literal worst. I felt like the worst mom. I felt like the worst wife. In all actuality, I felt like the worst human. I didn't feel like I was having the same experience that every other mom before me must have had... especially because there were people out there who willingly did this more than once. I loved Clark undoubtedly, but I didn't yet love being his mom or a mom, period[1].

When I was pregnant, there was lots and lots and <u>lots</u> of baby talk. Every conversation always focused on how I was feeling or looking in carrying this little one, what I should or shouldn't be doing while carrying this little one[2], or how excited folks were to meet this little one. The people in my life, it seemed, didn't avoid the topic of pregnancy or parenting, they just didn't get *really* real with me. During those pregnancy days, I heard a lot about the glories of newborns and parenting. I heard a lot about the "blessings" and the sunny moments and the highs of it all. What I *didn't* hear about, however, was the crash that promptly follows those highs. While others were quick to tell me about how wonderful and colorful becoming a parent would be, they weren't as quick to tell me that, sometimes anyway, it would be ugly, messy, hard, and scary-as-crap, too.

I struggled with my thoughts big time on the inside, but beyond some obvious moments of frustration and fatigue, they remained internal. Even my husband was left in the dark because, quite frankly, I was appalled at myself. For those of you who know Jonathan, you know that he is just about the nicest person in the world. I'm talking nice to the point that there have been times when I've actually gotten mad at him for being too nice as this makes me look or feel like a complete fill-in-the-blank just for having a whiny, selfish, and human moment. Ha. Nothing I could have ever thought or said would have made him love me less or think any less of me as a mother or wife. I can say this with certainty now, and I'm sure that I knew it then, but the fog of fatigue paired with the embarrassment I was afraid to feel in coming clean was enough to keep me quiet and alone... at first, anyway. As I started to discover some cracks in my isolation, however, I suspected that perhaps I wasn't so horrible of a person after all.

Fortunately for me, I'm usually not a bottler of feelings or one to hide what's going on in my world even when it's ugly, hence, this book. Except for when I am feeling super mature (sarcasm) and "handle" one of the occasional disagreements in my marriage with the silent treatment or the You Should Know What I'm Thinking game, it typically doesn't take me long to say what's on my mind. As a child, I most often got in trouble for talking back to my dad or inserting myself in the middle of an argument between my parents. As an adult, I can even be honest to a fault, at times. Well, true to form, as I slowly emerged from the fog of brand-spanking-new parenthood, I began to call bull on the idea that I was alone in my thinking.

In order to test the waters and figure out if I was the only beyond-awful parent out there with such thoughts, I started by putting little feelers out to my nuts-and-a-half sisters who reproduce like it's their job, Alicia and Ashley. At the time, Alicia had three children (ages six, five, and two... and would have twins almost exactly a year later), and Ashley had four (ages eight, six, three, and one). I didn't share anything too ugly or revealing because I didn't want to be the only one who was anything less than an A+ on the Mom Spectrum, but I did allow myself to be real-er, in tiny steps. Instead of "I thought this was going to be amazing and it's actually kind of the worst gig ever," which is what I was really thinking, I played it a tad safer and would say things like "Was this *this* hard for you guys, too?" You know what I got back from my older, Supermom sisters? "<u>Totally</u>. Still is!"

Since I didn't end up feeling embarrassed or isolated when I approached my sisters, I added my mom to the mix. My sisters may be pretty awesome, but my mom is the Supermom of all Supermoms. Like Jonathan, she is annoyingly nice (kisses, Mom!) and basically raised my sisters and I as a single parent while working a full-time job, cooking dinner every evening, and showing up at every single stupid dance recital, volleyball game, or National Honor Society induction. Mom's response? "Yep—me too!" (In fact, I think she said something more along the lines of... "I missed my old life and wanted it back." Amen, Mom!) Slowly, but surely, I was turning the corner on hiding from and with my very non-storybook feelings regarding motherhood and the newborn days. I realized that I had my mom and sisters in my corner, at least, and that they had been in the place I presently was.

It was right around this time that I sent out an email to my coworkers with some updates on Clark along with the obligatory, cute baby photos. He had been exceptionally fussy that morning and wanted nothing to do with anything other than me holding him. When I *finally* managed to get him to sleep for a whole five minutes outside of my arms, I parked myself at my computer to type a quick message and check in at work. I was tired, hadn't yet showered, and was already yearning for Jonathan to get home from work even though it was like ten in the morning. I can't recall the exact text, but I basically said something along the lines of:

- "I am reminding myself to enjoy *all* of the moments, even those filled with Clark's cries, because I know he will only need me for so long".

How eloquent and BS'y, right? I know myself well enough. Here's what I was actually thinking:

- "Can someone please drop me a venti caramel macchiato right about now because I can't even handle this day. I love Clark so much, but holy crap! Here are a few pictures that will fool you into thinking motherhood is always enjoyable, that I have a content baby, and that all is well in my world."

Much better. In some ways, I think this email was a bit of self-talk and personal therapy as much as it was anything else. I think I was hoping that if I put it in writing, it would be a self-fulfilling prophecy... or at least a good reminder. Maybe, it would give me some encouragement to enjoy the day, not just survive it as sometimes happens in the world of a new parent.

Well, my coworkers? They got the message. They adored the pictures[3], and they responded. And responded. And responded. The majority of the responses I received were expected and put-together, kind of like the gag-worthy message of mine that prompted their returned communication in the first place:

- "What a precious little boy!"
- "Enjoy your time at home!"
- "You all look so wonderful!"
- Barf, barf, barf...[4]

One response, however, was much lengthier than the others and, in the best way possible, slapped me right across the face... exactly when I needed it to.

Carey, the sender, shared that when she became a new mom, she worked hard to make herself look happy and perfectly in love to onlookers. Folks would ask how things were going, and her answer? "Great!" Just like me, however, motherhood wasn't at all what she had anticipated, and it left her feeling like a bad mom. One day, a friend of Carey's popped over for a visit and asked how life as a new mother was treating her. Before Carey could even get out the signature response, her friend looked her in the eyes and gave her this gold:

- "It *sucks* sometimes, doesn't it?"

When these words freed her to understand that she wasn't alone, abnormal, or awful at all, Carey stood in her kitchen and cried tears of relief with her friend... and when I read this email, questioning whether or not what my own loved ones and I were admitting to feeling reached beyond just our family, I also cried. I cried because I felt understood. I cried because I felt normal again.

At this point, the blinders were off and I started to get really real. On what has become an ongoing group text between my mom, sisters, and I[5]— a place where we laugh at each other, roll our eyes at one another, share prayer requests, and just keep it oh, so real—I probably said more horrible things than good things some days in the beginning simply because I finally felt like I could without being judged or ashamed. What I *never* got were responses of surprise or disgust. What I *always* got were responses of empathy, mutuality, and strengthened camaraderie. I thought that being honest would be embarrassing or isolating, but instead I found myself closer to those I could "come clean" to.

After having kept my feelings hidden during Clark's first weeks of life, a time that was so, so hard because it was just demanding, depleting, and different, I vowed never to put myself in that place again. I vowed to allow myself any and every thought and feeling that crossed my mind should I ever have another child. I vowed to accept that I could be a good mom and still think that being a mom wasn't always awesome (because it's *totally* not).

Remember how I wondered why people even have children in the first place and was darn sure that I wouldn't be repeating the experience? Well, when Jonathan and I returned to the delivery room for the birth of our daughter, Annie, just 20 months after Clark was born, we were there on very willing terms. If you're one of the pregnant readers out there, you may be feeling a little scared or uncomfortable processing any or all of my reality. Take heart in what I just said. I chose to become a mommy again not long after finding myself in a not-so-nice place because I wanted to do it a second time. I knew it was going to be rough and real… but I *wanted* it again. I wanted to feel the high of creating new life and watching it take a breath for the first time. I wanted to see my sweet husband melt again as he held his brand new infant. I wanted my little boy to experience life with a backup singer. I also wasn't completely opposed to being showered with 98 casseroles one more time…but, I digress. Guys, I wanted all of these things even knowing that there were lots of other, less desirable, things headed my way.

In the beginning, there's a pretty good chance you're going to feel just like my own mom felt when parenthood was new, and different, and nothing like she had expected. She missed her old, predictable, self-centered, dependent-free life… and you will too. You won't miss it all the time, thankfully, but when you do, you'll miss it deeply. You'll long for the simplicity of those before-baby days. The days when you would come home from work to an empty, quiet house, and set up on the couch for just a few minutes to read the mail and catch a bit of Ellen before starting dinner prep. Dinner that would be eaten hot, as anticipated. Dinner that could actually be savored, and not inhaled. Yep. Those days. You'll miss them, and at times, you'll want them back.

On the flip side of the coin, however, is the reality that while you'll miss your old life, you'll very quickly discover yourself in a place where your new life, diapers and all, is a much sweeter life. It's a much more purposeful, meaningful life. Before you know it, your sweet baby will become so embedded and ingrained in your everyday (every second) living, that you won't be able to, nor would you even want to, imagine life without him or her. Life with a child is a harder life and a more demanding life, for sure, but it's also a richer life worthy of every sacrifice.

Today, I can hold my head high and own all of the ugly and isolating things I thought in the difficult days after the births of my children, especially my firstborn. Discovering that I didn't love every moment of parenting, that being a mom didn't always feel like a blessing, and that the sunshine-y expectations I had of life with a newborn were pretty far from the realities I experienced? Well, all of this was normal and OK. What I came to realize through hiding my thoughts and feelings was that this left me feeling like the crappiest of people and the exact opposite of the kind of mom I had hoped to be. The second time around, by giving myself grace and sharing my yuck more readily, I enjoyed those first days and weeks more than I thought possible. Given the reality of the things dripping from my body and the sleep I certainly wasn't having, owning the awful bits of bringing home my baby the second time around made the beautiful bits so much sweeter.

---

1. I was able to put this thought to words with help from a former co-worker and mommy friend, Jill. When I saw Jill for the first time after she gave birth to her son, Kaden, I asked how things were going and got an <u>awesome</u>, candid answer. Her response? "I love Kaden, but I *hate* being a mom."

2. For the record, do NOT go to a home improvement store with the intention of independently purchasing bags of mulch while you are pregnant. I have never experienced so simultaneously hilarious and annoying of a situation ever before or since in my entire life. I literally had a stranger park her car next to mine and say to me, "You are *not* loading those bags into your car yourself, and I'm not moving until someone else does it for you." She wasn't kidding.

3. Seriously, though, how could they not? I mean, Clark was like half-smiling in the one shot and wearing a onesie that said "Mommy's Little Peanut". EEE!

4. I'm exaggerating here, of course, OV family! You know I loved and still love all of you and so appreciated your support and encouragement. I'm just saying we all kept it a little cliché and PC, if you know what I mean. Totally the way of the world.

5. Just for fun… Here are a few recent, real-life quotes from the Mom/Sis Group Text:
   - -"Life is all about making stupid choices, right?!"
   - -"Sugar is a food group too!"
   - -"I have no idea why I was so full, because all I can say is… microwaveable mashed potatoes."

- -"Come on Motrin, do your magic!"
- -"I'm sorry this is last minute, but is anyone willing to keep Annie alive for an hour?"
- -"Mommy, I know how to spell 'piss'!"
- -"I've never been summoned, but have always thought that jury duty might be a nice break from being a mom."

...How I love these women!

2 BODILY WRECKAGE

Pregnant? There's a pretty good chance I'm about ready to scare you again. Hang in there with me. I promise to bring some redemption to this chapter before it concludes. Let's all uncross our legs, put our chins up, and take a deep breath. You are stronger than you know!

Things I learned in childbirth class (Abridged Version):

- It's going to hurt.

- There are options to help lessen the hurt.

Things I *didn't* learn in childbirth class:

- Your lady bits may swell to a degree that an isolated photograph of said region shown to a stranger without context would result in a response of "What exactly am I looking at?"

- You will out-Hansel-and-Gretel even the most experienced of trailblazers. Bread crumbs? Who needs those! You'll be leaving behind a trail of drips, composed of a unique combination of bodily fluids, on the floor every time you walk anywhere wearing a hospital gown.

- Getting in and out of bed initially, let alone repositioning yourself, will hurt. Substantially. Imagine getting sucker punched down yonder, repeatedly, for like 45 minutes.

All kidding aside, childbirth classes are certainly helpful and do give you lots of important, good-to-know-ahead-of-time things to ponder. You'll laugh, but one of the takeaways I appreciated most from my own facilitator was a hands on encounter with the maternity maxi pads used at the hospital in which I planned to deliver. This probably doesn't seem like something one should appreciate or even remember, but let me just say that this helped remove a tiny bit of the shock factor from an encounter that was, at that point, a mystery to me. Seeing and holding a pad that was practically the size of a travel pillow gave me a little dose of reality in the mess that was to come. (If you haven't seen one of these suckers yet, holy crap— just wait. HUGE.) Along with many other wisps of wisdom and words of encouragement, childbirth classes provided a solid base of knowledge for my husband and I on which to start our next chapter. There are, however, just some things that you can't fathom about the experience until you've lived it.

For starters, saying that childbirth *hurts* is a little like saying ice is "cool". Nope. Ice is freezing, actually. Childbirth is a process that will require more than all of your mental, physical, and emotional strength. Want some transparency? When I was pregnant with Clark, I was all about portraying a perfect picture of pregnancy. I gained something like a measly 15 pounds from start to finish and ran almost every single day of that pregnancy, including the day Clark was born. (Before you gag, rest assured that my ego took a huge hit the second time around when I gained more than 50 pounds with Annie and experienced contractions any time I even *thought* about going for a run...) I decided early on that I was going to try my darndest to labor without medication, and while, yes, some of that decision was grounded in good-mom-intentions like I didn't want my child being exposed to drugs that weren't absolutely necessary, I'm just going to be frank yet again and tell you that I wanted the Drug-Free Badge of Accomplishment.

The early stages of labor were awesome for me with Clark because I was on my feet for an entire day (measuring the heights and weights of hundreds of Ore Valley Elementary School's kiddos as a school nurse) and distracted myself from the work my body was doing. While my colleagues were freaking out and pushing me to leave, I felt like I was in control and tarried on. I left around 3:30 PM after phoning Jonathan and met him at home shortly thereafter. While he was antsy and excited, I was very, weirdly chill at this point and probably experiencing a bit of denial. When he asked "Should we head into the hospital?", my response was "Nah. I think I want to take a hot shower first." I headed up the stairs and added a request, "Oh! And can you maybe make me a peanut butter and jelly sandwich[1]?" Although he looked concerned, Jonathan obliged with my plan, and off to the shower I went.

My husband is, and has always been, a rule follower to a "T". As a child, if he was given a chore to complete, it was done *immediately*. His brother, on the other hand... not so much...which drove Jonathan absolutely crazy (am I right, Justin?!?) When *I'm* in the kitchen, my philosophy is that a recipe serves as a guide. It is merely a suggestion, and I adapt. Always. When *Jonathan* is in the kitchen, he depends on a recipe like it's the instruction manual of an airliner he's been forced to commandeer after the pilot suddenly keeled over of a heart attack. He's cautious and thorough and has always been one to do what is right in any given situation. All things I love about him. Well, there was one "rule" that we were given in our childbirth class, and that was the rule of 5-1-1. When I was experiencing contractions at five or less minutes apart, lasting one minute, for at least one hour, I was supposed to head into the hospital. After my nice, l o n g shower and my couldn't-have-been-better PB&J, our conversation went like this (be forewarned that our pet names for one another are super original— "Boy" and "Girl"):

JONATHAN: So how far apart are your contractions?

ME: Dunno. Let's find out! OK, one is starting now...

Together look at clock

ME: And... time! Getting another.

JONATHAN: Girl! That was like two and a half minutes. We need to call the doctor and head in!

ME: Boy, I'm fine. They don't even hurt yet.

Well God has a sense of humor, because right around that time, my contractions started to hurt. We arrived at the hospital shortly before 6PM just shy of six centimeters dilated, and Clark arrived on the scene about three and half hours later. It wasn't like I nearly delivered him in the car or anything (shout out to my dear friend, Sue, to whom this actually happened!), but for a first child, my labor and delivery was brisk as compared to many. If it wasn't for this briskness, let it be known that I, Miss Fit, Miss I'm-Not-Taking-No-Drugs, would've been all *kinds* of doped up.

I handled labor with Clark like a champ until I got to the dreaded Transition Stage, as they call it. This is the final stage of dilation right before pushing in which contractions seem endless, and it is hard, hard, hard to maintain control over your pain... especially when you're a first time mom and have no idea what to expect. It was at this time when I cried Uncle! (the G-rated version of what I was actually thinking at the time) and told Jonathan that I needed him to get me some <u>drugs</u>. Jan, the super-experienced and best midwife who happened to be caring for me, knew that I wanted to deliver Clark "au naturale" but she wasn't unsympathetic to my agony. She came into my room, saw me spiraling out of control, and said to me, "You can do this, and I know you *want* to do this, but I'll call Anesthesia for you." She made the call (bless her soul!) and then told me that she was going to check my progress again to see where things stood.

Feeling completely defeated and like I had nothing left to give, Jan looked at me with a new brightness in her eyes and said, "Honey, you're ready to go! Your pain relief is going to be pushing." I'm not quite sure what escaped my lips at this moment, but let me just tell you that I wasn't looking forward to the "pain relief of pushing". Say what?!? I'm hurting beyond hurting, I'm about ready to drop a bowling ball from my bits, and you're telling me the only drug you've got for me is *pushing*?

As if all of the stars aligned and the light was changing from red to green, my body then did the weirdest thing ever: it involuntarily started pushing. Imagine that you've just chugged a bottle of laxative and are about to "bomb the porcelain sea" whether you make it to the toilet or not[2]. Yeah, it was a tad like that. How on Earth pushing a five to ten pound infant out of a ten centimeter canal could be considered pain relief is beyond me, but guess what... so true!

I put every ounce of my energy into pushing for almost 45 minutes in order to deliver Clark. While it certainly hurt, it was the first time in the laboring process where I felt like my pain was meaningful and pointed. There was light at the end of the tunnel (figuratively *and* literally...haha), and pushing was, in all truth, more exhausting than it was agonizing. Before we had Clark, Jonathan's sweet Grandma Dean once said this to me:

- "Wait until you hold that precious baby in your arms. All of the pain of delivery will just go away…"

True, Grandma, but only because of your careful phrasing. Yes, yes, absolutely yes, my pain was gone the minute I held Clark in my arms. Did I forget the pain, however? No, ma'am. I remember my best friends, Kelly and Megan, visiting me in the hospital the day after Clark's arrival and asking me how painful it really was. Unlike my hidden, yuck feelings that we already discussed… I was honest with this one from day one. I think my response was something like, "Oh my gosh it was BADDDD." Ha. Encouraging, right?

When I found out that I was pregnant the second time… I won't lie… I was more scared of delivery because I *did* know what to expect. Because I had given Clark a medication-free delivery, I really wanted to attempt that for his sister… and I was nervousssss. Keep it real? I felt especially driven to deliver Annie without drugs and give her at least one thing to be proud of me for during the time I carried her, because I basically did everything else wrong. I exercised ZERO, ate a ton of crapola, forgot to take my pre-natal vitamin like 50% of the time, and just didn't follow the rules the second time around like I had the first. Lunchmeat? Let me at it! (sorry, Annie-girl!)

Regardless of the why, I knew that I wanted to attempt a med-free delivery again, so I made it a point to do a little preparation in the form of research and prayer. For countless days, I prayed that God would give me the physical strength and mental clarity I would need to go where I didn't really want to go again. Somewhere along the line, I discovered a three word phrase that, although I initially hated, I would grow to love and rely upon. It was this:

- "Embrace your contractions!"

Simple in theory, yes, but quite the opposite in reality. Let's be honest… had Jonathan attempted a pep-talk during my labor with Clark by saying

"Come on, Girl. Embrace your contractions," I probably would've told him where to shove it. Pain is, well—painful—and anything but welcome. When the body experiences pain, the natural tendency is to fight the discomfort and find relief. Not exactly a warm and inviting "embrace". When a woman fights her contractions, as I did with Clark, their efficiency is lessened to a degree, and while the process of labor certainly continues, it isn't as fluid as it could be. Not easy to do, mommies-to-be, but if you need one thing to hold onto when you want nothing more than for your baby to just GET HERE ALREADDDDDY, here it is: Let your body do what it needs to do. As much as you can, which will at times feel impossible—r e l a x. Breathe. You've got this. Your body was created to do this hard, hard work.

While it was anything but easy, laboring with Annie was easier than it had been with Clark because of my determination not to fight and resist the pain. The process mirrored that of Clark's delivery almost identically except that I owned my contractions. When a contraction would start, I made it a point to relax every muscle in my body. I relaxed my face, my hands, my breathing, my everything... and I focused on the pain for the right reasons. I wasn't begging for it to leave. I was willing for it to be useful. Until basically the Transition Phase, I was happy, in control, and strangely talkative. When the Transition Phase came, that familiar hurt, hurt, hurt definitely returned, but I wasn't afraid of it. I allowed my body to do its thing, and on top of the Drug Free Badge of Accomplishment, I vowed to receive the Didn't-Even-Ask-for-Them-This-Time-Around Badge. I did it, friends.

As the pain peaked and I knew that I would soon get to experience the welcomed "relief" of pushing, my body again started doing it all on its own. The midwife entered the room donning her gloves in response to my husband's SOS call, and jets of amniotic fluid literally shot out of me hitting Jonathan and anyone else within a three foot radius of my nethers (it was kind of awesome). One and a half big ol' pushes later, and there was my sweet girl, Annie.

Expecting? First of all, you CAN do it. Second, it's totally OK if you don't want to do it—either from the get-go, or because the process becomes harder than you had imagined. You do you, and don't let anyone make you feel any less worthy whether you choose to medicate or go without. Your body is about ready to do the craziest, hardest, most amazing thing. Nothing can, or should, take away from that.

Just like we all know bringing home a baby is "hard", we all know that delivering a baby is going to "hurt". Regardless of how a baby makes the leap from womb to world (if only it was that easy...), and regardless of what medications are or are not used, even first-time parents anticipate a certain level of discomfort both during and after delivery. What I certainly didn't expect, however, was just *how much* labor and delivery would hurt along with a bunch of simply-weird realities regarding the aftermath of the entire experience.

First, for those blessed with uncomplicated, "typical" deliveries, like me, it's pretty weird how quickly things just normalize (or, at least, are expected to normalize). Without an epidural, there are next to no restrictions in movement during delivery or recovery. If you're medically stable and feeling up to it, you can essentially be on your feet, going to the bathroom, showering, and attempting to beautify your w r e c k e d self shortly after giving birth. Even with an epidural or a C-section, we are talking mere hours until a new mom is expected to be up and moving around independently. It may be natural, but giving birth is still traumatic-as-heck to a woman's body.

It's all kinds of crazy that our bodies do what they do during the delivery process and are then expected to carry on like nothing happened. Have you ever seen one of those stereotypical wildlife shows? After the zebra gives birth, she just lays around while her cohorts acknowledge the stress she's endured, bring her the best of the best whatever-zebras-eat, and allow her to rest while they care for the whatever-baby-zebras-are-called, right? Um, NO. Momma Z drops said baby in the dirt while munching on dinner, cleans the yuck off of her newborn with her own mouth (so gross, nature) and then moves on to whatever-zebras-do-all-day while baby Z follows along.

The reality of having a baby to care for is that suddenly there is no time for selfishness. Here's some honesty again, guys: after you've done the hard work of labor, you're going to want to be a little selfish. You're going to want that nap in the worst way. You're going to want to have a few minutes to laze in your filth without concern for the 700 visitors lining up outside your door. When they start making their way in, though... you're probably even going to want a couple (dozen) of them to tell you how amazing of a job you just did.

The nurses who cared for me during labor and delivery were all wonderful people whom I trusted myself and my children to completely. For this reason, please don't take what I am about ready to say as a dig at any of them in any way. Because I had such run-of-the-mill experiences, I was basically ignored unless I sought out attention for the duration of the process, with the exception of whatever was minimally required in monitoring and assessment. My medical team was gracious enough to give me space to labor as I wanted, and gracious enough to give Jonathan and I space to figure out how to keep our new little peanuts thriving once they were born. When my nurses *did* have to pop in for their infrequent, brief assessments, though? Well, life totally sucked for a few short moments. For those of you who have yet to experience childbirth, here are two dreaded words for you: uterus checks.

After delivery, it's essential that a woman's uterus remain firm and contracted, not only so that the womb can get "back into shape", but to prevent bleeding. To ensure that this is happening (or to encourage it *to* happen, if not), postpartum nurses have the responsibility of performing occasional checks of the uterus which involve rather-indelicately jamming their fingers into a woman's already-tender belly flesh in order to *intentionally* cause contractions in a super-sore organ that has been through the wringer (a heartfelt apology to each of the women that I, personally, had to do this to as a nursing student... so sorry!). Very necessary, but very uncomfortable, too.

If you're lucky enough to have boring (in a good way) deliveries, like me, and only see your nurses a couple of times during your hospital stay, believe me when I say your heart will skip a beat (in a bad way) any time you hear someone medical tell you they need to check you out below the belly button. Thankfully, these cringe-worthy check ins are few (yet somehow undoubtedly as soon as you doze off or baby is uncharacteristically quiet), and it will seem just plain weird how very little medical attention you receive considering what your body has been through.

Want to know what else is weird? The mess. Remember those travel-pillow-sized maxi pads? Oh yes, girl, you're going to need them. In the beginning, you're going to need like one every *hour*. Your bits will be so swollen, you'll be all kinds of sore, and you'll be trying to master the art of "comfort" (or at least tolerance) while sitting delicately on monster-sized cold packs. Going to the bathroom without making a complete mess of the floor, the toilet, or your underwear (*DON'T* even try using your own. For real. Suck it up and use the wonderfully-flattering, super-sexy, mesh disposables that the hospital provides. They're there for a reason!) for at least the first 24 hours will be impossible.

There are literally stages of drainage down below that a woman goes through after delivering a baby. It's like the heaviest, longest, grossest period of your entire life. Here's a quote that made me laugh out loud and nod my head like "Yep!" all at the same time having experienced this messy ride twice now. It comes from Cleveland Clinic and addresses the drainage after birth, which is called lochia: "Lochia for the first three days after delivery is dark red in color. A few small blood clots, no larger than a plum, are normal."[3] I don't know what kind of plums you all are eating, but I'm not sure that I'd exactly consider a plum small... especially when we are talking about their size in comparison to a blood clot being passed from one's body and considered to be "normal". I mean, if we are comparing them to watermelons, sure, I guess perhaps a plum is small. Anyway, welcome to all kinds of new "normals"!

While the degree of the overall gross factor following childbirth caught me by surprise and provides for many humorous memories today, my favorite, favorite post-delivery "what the what?!? moment" involves yet another simply-weird reality:

- *Things will be different down South.*

If you haven't heard it already, mommies-in-the-making, you'll hear it 30 times in the hospital prior to discharge: Be sure not to insert anything into the vagina (alas, the V word makes its debut) for at least six weeks following delivery and until cleared to do so by a medical provider. Remember my husband, the rule follower? This was not going to be challenged. Easy enough, right? Well, as I healed at home during the first several weeks following Clark's birth, I couldn't help noticing that stuff just felt "different". Things were bulgy, and I felt some tightness, but I just chalked it up to the normal process of recovery.

One day, however, my curiosity got the better of me. The discharging doctor may have told me not to *insert* anything down there, but she never told me I couldn't *look*. While Clark napped, I placed a mirror on my bathroom floor, hunkered over the thing, and then ran to call Jonathan at work.

ME: Boy, something is NOT RIGHT. You need to come home over lunch.

JONATHAN: Umm, what? Are you OK? Is Clark OK?

ME: Yes, we're fine, but something is NOT RIGHT with my lady parts.

JONATHAN: What do you mean?

ME: There's something *there*. There's something there that wasn't there before.

JONATHAN: Umm. OK? Does it hurt? Should I come home now?

ME: No, it's fine. Just come home over lunch. I don't feel like it's supposed to look like this…

Hahaha. What a call to receive at work, and what a lunchtime request. My sweet, concerned husband showed up not long after this conversation. He was flustered, for sure, and uncertain of what he may find seeing as how my description of what was going on wasn't exactly thorough or scientific. Upon further inspection, without breaking the cardinal rule of *insertion*, the hubs described to me that there was a band of skin literally connected to both sides of my girly tunnel. TMI, I know… (so sorry!) but he could literally hook his finger around the thing and pull. It was substantial and wasn't going anywhere. Totally gross.

I promptly called the OB/GYN office, and, comically, I was chided like a toddler:

SASS-PANTS RECEPTIONIST: You do *know* that you aren't supposed to insert anything into your vagina for a full six weeks after delivery, correct?

ME: Yes, I do. I didn't *insert* anything. I looked.

SPR: And you're sure this wasn't there before?

ME: Um, yes. I'm not sure how a rubber band connecting the walls of my vagina would still be intact after giving birth.

SPR: Well, as long as it isn't painful, you already have your six week visit scheduled in a few weeks' time. The midwife will take a look then.

ME: OK. As long as you aren't concerned, that's fine with me.

SPR: And *remember*. Make sure you don't insert anything into your vagina before that appointment.

ME: Roger, chief! (Ha. This was what I *wanted* to say. I actually just said something more like "Yep. I know!")

What we came to learn at that appointment was that I had an adhesion, tissue which had grown in response to the way I was sutured after delivery. It was totally normal and totally non-concerning, but the midwife wanted to "cut it down", as was her description, right then and there without medication. I know that I had just delivered a child sans drugs, but let me tell you that after you've experienced significant pain in the South of France, you will do anything to avoid recurrence without time to prepare yourself and get in the zone. Thankfully, Jonathan came along for that appointment and convinced the midwife to jack me up with a numbing agent before she came at me with a scalpel. Thank you, love. Another reason why you're my favorite!

All things considered, I think it's pretty safe to say that labor, delivery, and recovery is a beyond challenging and super weird process. It'll leave your body completely wrecked and exhausted, a dripping mess, and forever different below the belt. I know, I know… I'm just making it all sound awful again, especially to the pregnant readers out there, but we've got to remember the *whole* picture. Thankfully, there's more to it than the "ick" and the "ouch".

For every ounce of pain that comes along with childbirth, there is a pound of exhilaration. Becoming a parent is hard-earned… like *really* hard-earned… and perhaps it takes such effort and results in such change as a way to reveal to us just how capable we are and how malleable we need to be. It's in this awkward and messy place that I first experienced a love so real I could almost touch it. It's where I discovered a love so strong, it hurt in a beautiful way. The tiny fingers wrapped around my own? The swaddled baby whose entire body could fit nestled on my chest? I wouldn't trade the pain I endured, the clothing I stained, or the pelvic floor I basically destroyed (jogging and peeing are now companion activities in my life!) for any of it. My thinking is this: the more you expect the mess, the more you can enjoy the wonder.

---

1. There are few things better in life than a good old PB&J. Seriously. My husband can attest that I would willingly eat these sons-of-guns for dinner every night if I didn't have other peoples' palates to please...
2. Need some laughs? Please...right now... perform the following Google search just as I did in order to complete the sentence that coincides with this footnote: "slang terms for going poop". You won't regret it.
3. "Pregnancy: Physical Changes After Delivery." *Cleveland Clinic*, 10 Mar. 2016, https://my.clevelandclinic.org/health/articles/physical-changes-after-delivery.

3   EXHAUSTION BEYOND EXHAUSTION

Sleep has always been my friend. OK, maybe my *best* friend (sorry, Kell!). Unlike my hubby, I am a napper, and I can fall asleep just about *any*where... at *any* time... wearing *any*thing. Or at least I was, in the BC era: Before Clark. Prior to parenthood, if Jonathan would travel on a work-related trip, my idea of a bangin' evening was splurging on a pint of ice cream and a massive bowl of popcorn in front of the TV before hitting the pillow at like 9. I was never a night owl, nor was I an early bird. I was more like a 10 AM to 2 PM kind of girl... followed by, what else? A nap. I knew that having children meant sacrificing sleep. Remember my crazy sisters and their 600 children? I saw them looking a little haggard each time a wee one was born, and I heard them snicker if I complained of being tired myself. I surface-level-knew that babies were time consuming and demanding at all hours of the day.

The moment I became a mom, however, is the moment I *knew* exhaustion (Amen, parents?). I hadn't been sleeping well for weeks because of being the Hump-belly of Notre Dame, plus I had just performed the workout of my life during labor and delivery, and I now had to consider a precious and helpless little one that depended heavily on me. As the first moments rolled into the first hours, which then rolled into the first days and weeks of Clark, I understood the snickers of my sisters. I also understood why, not only once... but *twice*... my brother-in-law, Joe, cross-dressed his male and female twins in their first days. The best part of it all? He probably wouldn't have even noticed and had to be told by Alicia that Zander wasn't exactly a "Cute Little Sister" nor was Julia "Mommy's Handsome Guy". I already think all of you out there expecting or currently parenting multiples are saints, but those of you with opposite-sex babies? Having to put effort into thinking about two completely separate wardrobes has to extra-suck. I feel you, Joe. Just like you were in those early baby days, I was *tired*.

Shortly after I had delivered Clark, I received a brief window of alone time. While he was being bathed for the first time, Jonathan went along to document the event behind a camera. One would think that I used this time to allow my totally-wrecked and completely spent body a chance to ask itself WTH?! and get some sleep, right? Hardly. Endorphins are like the "upper" of all uppers. I tried to process what had just happened and convince myself to rest, but my mind raced at 100 miles a minute. As became the trend of my hospital stay and the weeks to follow, the moment I finally settled down and began to drift off was the same moment that Daddy was wheeling Clark back into my room. Hello, boys!

It was around this time that we attempted to get Clark, who hadn't really fed yet, to figure out what to do with a boob. Our first encounters with breastfeeding were hardly successful as Clark preferred, at that point, to snooze...the one time when being awake would have been desired over sleeping. Because I really wanted to breastfeed and was working with a less-than-willing participant, we were introduced to what would soon become my mortal enemy: the breast pump. Listening to instructions on how to operate an unfamiliar device comprised of lots of separate, tiny pieces that require assembly, disassembly, and washing with every use at approximately 2 AM after having recently squeezed a melon from your insides is a little like trying to interpret a foreign film without subtitles. I saw the nurse's mouth moving. My ears heard words. My brain, however... not so much. For the next hour or so, Jonathan and I continued feeding attempts and got tangled up in tubes and incorrectly placed pump parts. I can only imagine how hopeless and hilarious we probably looked.

When we decided that it was time to call it a night, we laid our burrito belly up in his bassinet (Parenting win! We remembered something!), Jonathan curled up on the ultra-deluxe (ha) pull-out bed next to me, and I attempted to find a position that was tolerable enough not to bring discomfort to any of the 95 parts of my body that were sore. And then we all slept soundly for three hours until Clark needed to "eat" again... Or <u>not</u>.

Just as one cannot know exhaustion until he or she becomes a parent, one cannot know *worry* either. I don't mean this as a cut at men in ANY way, but I think this is especially true of moms. Genetically speaking, I truly believe women are wired to fret over the welfare of their children. It's in our bones, so to say. My husband is seriously like the Champion Dad of Dads— I don't think I changed a single diaper for either of my babies in the hospital, he's a freaking kid magnet whom all of my nieces and nephews prefer over me, and, unlike most men who need time to bond with their babies and prefer the later stages of parenting, this guy was *in it* from day one. Despite his proclivity for all-things-baby, I have lost far more sleep than Jonathan has in the years since welcoming our children into the world simply because I *worry* about them and hear e v e r y single noise that they mutter in their sleep.

The first night in the hospital, if any part of Clark moved a fragment of a centimeter, I knew about it. I quickly learned that even as they slumber, babies aren't quiet. They rustle a lot, they grunt, and, weirdly, they sneeze. I remember actually calling my nurse in the wee hours of the morning because Clark sneezed so often that I wondered if it was possible he had somehow fallen ill already[1]. After convincing myself that if I ever wanted to sleep again I was going to have to drown out these sounds and trust that staring at Clark wasn't what was keeping him breathing (SO hard the first night, guys!), I may have gotten a solid ten minutes of shut eye before it was time for one of the infrequent, yet somehow always inconveniently timed, medical interruptions.

And so began the new "normal" of never really reaching a point of deep sleep and having to achieve it, instead, in all-too-short bursts. Not exactly restful or rejuvenating, especially for someone who loves sleep (or used to, anyway) so very much. Whether it was my peanut crying for his needs to be met (which felt like *all* the time) or the constant presence of visitors wanting to get their hands on some bitty baby, there were very few opportunities for anything resembling sleep in the hospital. Once we got home, though, Jonathan, Clark, and I slept like bosses. Just kidding.

Coming home from the hospital was both a stress-relieving and stress-inducing experience. While we were so super ready to be in our own home with our own "stuff", there was also this nagging sense of anxiety that we carried through the doors with us. It was like... "What do we do now?" Anyone who knows me knows that I am a planner. Seriously, I've got to be among the planniest planners (yes, you read that correctly) to have ever graced God's green Earth. Ladies, has your man ever surprised you by showing up with takeout that he picked up on his way home from work? You know, a cute and thoughtful gesture intended to keep you from having to slave away in the kitchen for an evening? True story, right hand to the Bible: Last night, my hubby comes walking through the door with a pizza box in hand. While I *should* have thought something resembling "Aww, that's so sweet of you!", especially because I *love* me some carb-laden pizza, my thoughts were a heck of a lot closer to (real life, guys...) "And what are we going to do with *that*?!?" Not in my plan.

I plan things like nobody else. I plan things that don't require planning. To illustrate, one of the things I often plan is a general flow of my caloric intake for the day (go ahead, roll your eyes... I totally, 300%, deserve it). For example, if I know I'm going to want to nosh on something salty and savor a giant bowl of ice cream once my kiddos are in bed for the evening, I try to balance the not-so-good food decisions by eating a healthier, less calorie dense, dinner. Guess who didn't have pizza last night? *This* girl. Haha! It's probably diagnosable, but I thrive on routine and predictability. Wanna know what the furthest thing from a predictable routine is? Life with a newborn.

The first night home from the hospital with Clark, I was tired (*tired*, TIRED, <u>tired</u>, **tired**... you get the picture) and thought for sure that I'd be able to get a few hours of sleep, even if they were staggered. I was tired enough, in fact, that I thought I might be able to tune out Clark's little sounds, sneezes and all. Sneezing, however, wasn't the bodily function that caused an issue that first night at home. What was the culprit, you may be asking? Hiccups.

If hiccuping was a paid occupation, both of my babies would have been millionaires within the first month of their lives. Initially, these little squeaks are oh-so-cute and just make you want to squeeze your tiny, smushy, babe...but believe me, guys, they're not so adorable at 3 AM when they cause your wee one to spit up and choke, send you into a full-blown, hormonal freakout, and result in you calling your sister so that together, she and your deliriously exhausted husband can convince you to step down off the ledge. Yup. That happened. In a display of sisterly love, Ash had encouraged me to call her at any time after coming home should I need anything. Bet she didn't expect me to take her up on that offer so soon... I think we made it a whole nine hours from the time we crossed our threshold until I placed my panicked SOS.

Just as "finally falling asleep when it was time to wake up for one reason or another" became the trend of *my* life early on, "requiring the completion of a multistep process in order to achieve any sort of slumber" became *Clark's*. From the beginning, I suspected that Clark was going to be somewhat of a "high maintenance" infant, especially when it came to falling asleep (Annie proved this inkling true when she arrived, by the way... SO much easier). Clark may have been a fairly-solid snoozer once he fell asleep and did gift Jonathan and I immensely with sleeping through the night way (WAY way) earlier than his sister, but the getting to sleep part was always the culprit with this boy. He was never the type of baby capable of putting himself to sleep, even with a full belly. Unless we wanted to listen to the incessant cries of our guy when he was tired, Jonathan and I were required to provide lots of rocking, bouncing, snuggling, swaddling, pacifying, and shushing. When the vibrating feature on Clark's bassinet died one evening, we even mastered the skill of rocking that sucker with our feet while semi-sleeping (victory!).

To this day, nap time and bedtime with Clark, although super endearing, nearly necessitate the use of an instruction manual. My firstborn is far from simple, to say the very least. He requires dimmed lighting, a white noise machine, his two current favorite stuffed animals, a pile of security blankets, two stories, a prayer, a specific song, a kiss on the lips and a blown kiss from the door, along with reminders that no smoke and no dragons (???, hahaha) are going to enter his room at night and that his alarm clock will light up at "seven zero zero" AKA 7 AM[2]. OCD much?

I'm picking on my bud a bit here, but this is all true. Would you like to know what else is true? I told you I'd be honest, so honest I'll be. Today is not an A+ day in the momming world. As I type this, I am very literally sitting here with a sore throat from yelling at Clark just minutes ago as he fought, and fought, and fought me to go down for a nap. I guess not much has changed with this kiddo in the high maintenance department. Most nights in the beginning, it felt like the amount of time it took just to settle Clark and convince him to sleep anywhere other than our arms (we *totally* fell asleep with him on our chests, in bed, on multiple occasions, which is not at all safe) far surpassed the amount of time he, or we, actually slept. Every night felt like a never-ending cycle of sleeplessness that just spilled over into an exhausting day.

If you're pregnant or are a brand-new parent, I am willing to bet money that you've heard the following tip *many* times before:

- "Sleep when baby sleeps"

While I did find this advice to be beneficial to a degree, I also found it annoying and mostly unhelpful for a variety of reasons revolving around four basic principles: Cooking, cleaning, grooming, and feeding. Let's investigate these ideas together.

1. Cooking.

Folks will tell you that cooking can be removed from the to-do list getting in the way of rest for new parents because loved ones will bring use amounts of food (this is a typo and should say "mass amounts", but it made me giggle so much that I decided to leave it for your reading pleasure… large amounts of food do lead to large amounts of derrière, after all, so I'm going to say it's fitting and appropriately incorrect). Yes, if you're blessed with super supportive and want-to-lighten-your-load friends and family members like Jonathan and I are, they will. It's true that you may find yourself freed from the chore of planning and preparing meals initially. Why is this in any way a problem, and how might it limit your ability to sleep during the day, you may be asking? Well, most of the time food drop-off comes with a visit (we'll spend an entire chapter on the concept of visitors soon enough), and if you're a tad OCD like I am (perhaps Clark's bedtime rituals can be explained through genetics?), you and your house may not want to look like utter crap when someone who has gotten a *whole lot* more sleep than you in recent days shows up on your doorstep with bright eyes, a mammoth lasagna, and a mission to snuggle a baby. This leads us to concepts two, three, and four.

2. Cleaning.

Housework can wait. I get this, and I support it wholeheartedly. Most of the time, however, even a brand-new, exhausted, and struggling mom feels the need to keep her "nest" tidy to an extent. This might not be *as* true if said momma is living in complete isolation, but isolation when a wee one is welcomed is seldom the case. Babies=Visitors. Hey guys, if you're ever coming over for a visit and you tell me you don't care what state my house is in… please know that I believe you, and I appreciate what you've said, but, quite frankly, it doesn't matter that *you* don't care. *I* care. It's just in my DNA.

3.   Grooming.

I'm sure that there are people out there who leave the hospital after giving birth feeling like a million bucks, but guess who didn't. Um, me! Regardless of how much weight you do or don't gain during pregnancy, it takes a while for your body to "bounce back". Most post-baby bodies look kind of like half-pregnant-but-whole-tired, swollen, uncomfortable forms of the woman affected prior to gestation. Because of this, it becomes necessary for us lady folk to highlight the good things we have going for us instead of accentuating the not-so-good…especially when we know we've got some kind stranger from church, who could potentially look all-sorts-of-put-together, bringing us a pot roast in a few short hours. How do we achieve this? Here are some ideas, ordered by the amount of effort required on the part of our new mom from least effort to most effort:

- Dressing oneself in a loose-fitting, yet flattering outfit that is actually chosen from a drawer. You heard me, girls. The floor, the hamper, and/or the clothing you "slept" in last night are *not* options.
- Showering oneself daily. Oh yes, mommies-to-be, even bathing once a day will require you to muster energy from the depths of your core. It's going to happen. I promise.
- Primping oneself in any way, shape, or form. This includes the use of *any* hair product, the application of makeup to *any* degree (Chapstick included!), or putting on *any* piece of jewelry.

Accentuating the not-so-good is easy. Sweatpants for days, shower when (overly) smelly, and, in the words of Sweet Brown[3], "ain't nobody got time for" earrings. Highlighting the good, however, is loads more challenging, loads more time-consuming, and not always feasible if we "sleep when baby sleeps".

4. Feeding

Babies sleep *a lot*, right? Hence folks telling us to "sleep when baby sleeps" in the first place. My argument on this one, however, is that babies sleeping *often* and sleeping *a lot* aren't really one and the same. In the next chapter, you're going to learn enough about my boobs and their mission to breastfeed to last you a lifetime. For a new mom to keep her new baby thriving, baby's gotta eat...like ALL THE TIME. In the beginning especially, just about the time you've wrapped up one round of feeding, changed the inevitable three poopy diapers (before, during, and after feeding was always the course for my babes), and gotten baby down for a nap, it's time to start it all again (Multiples, you say? O M G, you guys, you deserve a Medal of Honor.). You know who else needs nutrition? Oh, right... you! After all, the casseroles (see concept one) are piling up in the fridge and someone has to eat them, right?! Even without breastfeeding, a parent needs to eat just to have the energy to make it through the day. With *lactation*, however, we're talking crazy caloric needs... more so than you even needed to grow that baby in the first place. Being a parent often means putting one's own needs in the backseat in order to meet the demands of our dependent infants, toddlers, and children. I can't even tell you how many times I've looked at the clock since my kids arrived and thought to myself "Hmm. I don't think I drank anything all day today. Oh, and did I eat lunch?" Bottom line: keeping your very-new newborn fed takes So. Much. Time... and making sure your *own* needs are met on top of that? You get the picture.

You see, there's lots more to the story than "sleep when baby sleeps." If it was that simple, I think there'd be far fewer parents, moms and dads alike, looking so exhausted beyond exhausted those (sometimes *awful*) first days and weeks of parenthood. It's enough of a problem just to find the time to nap when life's demands, be it baby or otherwise, are shouting your name. If and when such sacred moments are found and utilized for rest, convincing a hormonal, run-ragged mind to shut down... not always the simplest of tasks.

If you were between the ages of two and ten in 1992, like I was, you will most likely recall the show Lamb Chop's Play-Along![4]. If you've *ever* seen it, you know the God-forsaken song for which it is known (and will now have stuck in your head for approximately ever). "The Song that Doesn't End"[5] is essentially the same phrase, repeated over and over and over and over again in a never-ending loop. This, friends, is how parenthood (especially the feeding parts) often feels in the beginning. Feed baby, change diaper, pray that everyone gets a little sleep. Repeat. Repeat. Repeat. Repeat. Repeat.

The first days at home with Clark were oh, so tiring and oh, so hard. I remember feeling utterly stuck in the depleting, cyclical "song that didn't end" in the beginning, so much so that I was actually jealous of my husband for being able to return to work and escape the monotony and fatigue. Getting to leave the house, without a baby, to talk to other adults, without having to worry about whether or not a certain dependent little nugget was hungry or tired or wet... all while sipping a cup of *hot* coffee? Yeah, man. I longed for it. Instead, I was cooped up at home, with a baby who couldn't communicate, and was always thinking about him and his many needs... all while sipping on a way-cold, brewed-five-hours-ago cup of coffee (*if* I even remembered that it was sitting on the counter). When you become a parent, gone are the days of fresh coffee or hot *anything*. Truth.

All of this is an exaggeration, of course. Jonathan is a hard, hard worker, with an important job as a Network Engineer that demands a lot of him. He may be able to sit at a desk or in a meeting the majority of a "typical" day, but it's not like he was twiddling his thumbs while I struggled at home. Lots of people depend on the work he does, or has done, to function in their day to day roles. When you're in the thick of the newborn fog, however, and you're wanting nothing more than a night of old-school, quality, uninterrupted sleep or maybe even like a measly *hour* of daylight time to do whatever-the-heck you want to do without consideration for anyone else, it's easy to slip into feelings of envy and resentment that can drive a wedge between partners who are actually at a point of needing one another more than ever before.

There is no way around the weariness that accompanies bringing home a newborn. Infants have to learn *everything*, including how to establish eating and sleeping patterns. All of this, as any parent knows, takes time, and patience, and monumental sacrifices in the slumber department for Mom and

Dad. Bypassing or ignoring the exhaustion? Impossible. Managing and surviving it, however? Yep, sure can.

For starters, in spite of and in response to those feelings of resentment for your spouse or your "other" that *will* surface… you've got to be real with one another. You've got to communicate openly and honestly, even when thoughts are anything-but-kosher, pretty, or rational. *Choose* to rely on your partner (or whoever your closest support person is) like you never have before. If you're like Jonathan and I, we tend to be fortunate in that when one of us is having a "moment" or reaching the end of our individual rope, the other is able to maintain composure and see the situation from a different, more sensible, vantage point. By allowing myself to *break* in front of my husband time and time again in the newborn days and admit to him that I needed help, I was able to get through some hard stuff a little more intact than I would have otherwise.

For those of you who are about to embark on the adventure of parenthood, the fatigue that awaits you is, truthfully, far beyond anything you can imagine. It's going to be so real. As I've said before and will say again, however, it's far from the entire story. For as tired as I was in becoming a mother, I was also never more in love. It took a few weeks, I won't lie, to adjust myself to this new "normal" and the demands that it entailed, but when the time rolled around for *me* to return to work, guess who wasn't jealous of Jonathan anymore. In fact, I was anything but. As it turns out, not one cell of my being was ready for that day, and oh, how absolutely devastated and heartbroken I was. I would've given just about *anything* for more time with my son, even the monotonous, draining, and opposite-of-glamorous parts… so much so that I tried (fruitlessly) to bargain with HR in order to make some sort of deal and buy myself a few more weeks. A lack of sleep has a way of making difficult things more difficult and ugly things more ugly. The beauty in what I was doing as a new mom was always there… it just took me a little while to see it through the fog.

---

1. If your baby happens to be a sneezer like mine, have no fear. This odd occurrence has nothing to do with illness and everything to do with the fact that newborns' respiratory systems are immature and trying to figure out what to do with air instead of amniotic fluid. Who knew?

2. Since writing this chapter a few weeks ago, we can now add even more to Clark's list of bedtime necessities. He now also requires us to assure him that he,

Jonathan, and I will "sleep good", a tissue at his bedside in case one is needed overnight, and a calculator on hand for quiet play when he wakes. According to his Grammy, for the record, he gets this from his Daddy. My mom says I was pretty easy. (Thanks, love.) Oh, Lord, help me with this boy…

3. "OKC Apartment Complex Catches Fire, 5 Units Damaged." *NewsChannel 4*. KFOR-TV, Oklahoma City, 8 Apr. 2012.

4. Lewis, Shari, creator. *Lamb Chop's Play-Along!* Paragon Entertainment Corporation, 1992-1995.

5. Norman Martin. "The Song that Doesn't End." 1988.

4   TALES FROM THE BOOB

Before we started together on the journey that is this book, I set out a list of caveats. For this chapter specifically, I think I need to lay down even more. Breastfeeding is just one of those buzz topics that makes people go *nuts*. There are proponents who will tell you that breastfeeding is the only way, that it *is* possible for all women with work, and that providing your infant with anything other than what nature intended is to rob that child of immunity-boosting antibodies unavailable elsewhere. There are others who find breastfeeding off-putting, gross, and even offensive[1]. Some women will run their bodies ragged, pay outrageous copays for frequent appointments with a lactation consultant, load up with milk-boosting supplements, teas, and even lactation cookies (yes, they exist) in order to breastfeed their little ones. Some, on the other hand, will elect a bottle from day one, basking in the option of shared responsibility in feeding (…let someone else handle a feeding or two overnight? YES!). Many women would love to breastfeed and cannot, while others prefer not to and have the ability to do so.

As a concept, breastfeeding is complicated and rather polarizing. While much of what *I* will speak to revolves around breastfeeding and pumping, please don't feel like an outsider if you are a past, present, or future formula-feeder. Keeping a newborn fed is exhausting, period. Further, please know that I am in no way pretending to be a lactation consultant or trying to take away from the amazing work that these women (and men, I suppose?) do. They are champions for something that is, in my opinion, beautiful and pretty amazing… and also holy-crap-hard, a monumental commitment on the part

41

of a mom, and simultaneously demanding and draining beyond explanation. Sounds like fun, right? Well, away we go!

Jonathan and I were talking with one of our best friends, Cody, a few months back about how fascinatingly backwards humans are as a species when it comes to babies. Think about it. We are the smartest and most evolved organisms on the face of the planet, yet our offspring are arguably the most helpless, dependent, and slow-to-develop. When it comes to mammals, in the vast majority of cases a mother gives birth to one or more babies, and within minutes, they instinctively figure out how to nurse and obtain milk. There isn't much of a learning process for Mom or Fluff-Ball. It simply happens. Just like I know there are parents out there who have experienced nothing but rainbows from the first moment of their bundle's existence, I am sure there are those whose experience with breastfeeding was much like the mammalian one I just described. Lactation consultants will tell you, after all, that when done correctly, breastfeeding should feel natural and be pain-free. Despite this, who would like to venture a guess at whose introduction to breastfeeding (both times around) felt quite the *opposite* of natural, easy, and comfortable. Mmm-hmm. Me!

If you're new to the world of breastfeeding, the "latch" is how a baby fastens itself to your milk makers. From the very beginning, Clark wasn't a good latcher and had little to no interest in my boob. I've always said it *this* way: Clark ate to survive. Unlike some babies who find comfort and experience lots of great bonding time while being nourished, my guy put forth the least amount of effort possible in order to meet his most basic of needs. For starters, because we were so enamored with his perfection and wanted to show him off to our loved ones as soon as possible, Jonathan and I missed out on the window of alertness that most babies experience immediately after birth as an opportunity for breastfeeding Clark. I kept myself covered so that everyone waiting next door could come say hello. I'll be the first one to admit that I waited too long, and I honestly think this encumbered later attempts. By the time I got around to trying breastfeeding with Clark, he was overstimulated and wanted (uncharacteristically) to sleep.

Further, my basic anatomy is far from an A+ when it comes to breastfeeding. If you're pregnant and never before considered the size, shape, and *length* of your nipples, the day is coming fast. Apparently, guys, I have short nipples. Short nipples and tiny mouths, I came to learn quickly, don't always add up to simple breastfeeding. Because Clark had little to latch onto and could've cared less whether or not he succeeded, my nurse recommended a "nipple shield" and added it to the mix. This multipurpose tool, which is completely explained in its own name… a thin piece of plastic that shields the nipple during feedings… served not only to protect my nipples from the "toughening up" that many women experience as newbies to breastfeeding, but also to add length to my vertically-challenged buttons.

The good news: Clark had more on which to latch. The bad news: everything else. Nipple shields are helpful, basic little buggers who bring with them a whole set of nonsense. First, albeit minimal, there's the added effort of having something to wash before and after every (frequent) feeding. Second, and still minimal, nipple shields can sometimes be a little drippy and messy. Third, and *very **NOT** minimal,* use of a shield results in the addition of a (insert twenty two expletives) breast pump.

When a newborn is put to the breast, the little tugs and pulls on a woman's nipples actually stimulate her brain to release hormones that aid in milk production, milk ejection, and the recovery process of the uterus (crazy cool, our bodies!). While the nipple shield certainly has its benefits, the artificial barrier that is created between an infant's mouth and a mother's skin inhibits nipple stimulation. End result? Pumping becomes necessary after every (I say again, *frequent*) feeding so that a new mom's body knows that it needs to keep producing and releasing breast milk.

Before we even get deep into the "glories" of pumping, let's just pause to spend a moment discussing the *logistics* of feeding a baby. Newborns have tiny tummies and super-new digestive systems. Basically, they require small amounts of food at frequent intervals because their bodies are learning, among so many other things, how to procure, process, and poop (I feel like that should be the slogan for something baby-related. Right?!). Generally speaking, I think most people know that babies have to be fed *often* regardless of whether or not they have, or ever plan to have, children. It's one of those things like knowing that having a baby means sacrificing on sleep or that labor "hurts".

On average, newborns have to eat every two to three hours. I remember learning this in my childbirth classes, and, before having any experience at all in the realm of breastfeeding, thinking that it sounded manageable. My line of thinking was something akin to the following two statements:

- "Oh ok! So I feed baby during the day and then have two to three hours to snuggle or get stuff done…"

OR

- "Oh ok! So I feed baby during the night and then have two to three hours to get some sleep…"

Let's all take a moment to collectively laugh at inexperienced, naive, me. HAHAHAHAHAHAHAHAHAHA.

Guess what? That two to three hour window we learn about… well it *includes* feeding time. Guess what else? In order to promote milk production in the best way possible, you've got to feed fully from one side and at least offer the second side with every (say it with me— FREQUENT) feeding. Take a stab at how long a full feeding is, initially. *Fifteen* to *twenty* minutes. Per. Side. Oh, and don't forget that you've got to burp baby in between sides and after you've (finally) finished. And sometimes baby will poop once, or twice, or three times during a feeding and require changing(s). And if your baby is on the smaller side like my two were, your pediatrician will likely push the *two* hour mark, especially during the day, and even emphasize that you *wake* baby at night to feed. And sometimes, be it day or night, baby is going to want to sleep through the whole thing so you're going to have to perform all sorts of ridiculous feats to keep him or her awake enough to receive nourishment[2]. We're talking cold washcloths, stripping baby naked, purposely trying to startle baby… yeah, it's totally mean stuff.

What does all of this craziness boil down to? Well, initially at least, it took me a solid 60 to 90 minutes from the time I started a feeding until I was able to high-five the hubs and say, "YES! (Anything but) Nailed it!"… only to look at the clock, realize that we'd be doing it all again oh, so very soon, and add "I take that high-five *back*. That took an hour? You've got to be kidding me!" Remember how we talked about pure and utter exhaustion in the last chapter? So real. Brand new parents are expected to feed their babies eight to 12 times a day. That's eight to 12 of the demanding, time-consuming cycles I just described.

Now that we're all on the same page as far as the basics of feeding a wee one *sans* breast pump, let's add in the "joy" of tacking on another 15 minute obligation immediately following every (established F-word) feeding. Pumping, in general, is a clumsy and cumbersome process, especially when you're inexperienced and taking it all in. Add into the mix your sleep deprivation and hot-mess hormones? You'll be feeling like a frustrated and completely-tired dairy cow in no time flat. Wanna know what else is super tough to swallow? In all likelihood, your milk won't even come in until you get home from the hospital, so many of these initial marathon-length feedings and subsequent pumping sessions will result in only minuscule amounts of milk being passed to your little one or dripped into a tube. (I know, I know, the lactation consultants out there are lighting their matches and about ready to toss this book onto the bonfire... but let's relax for just a second. Time for another collective cleansing breath. All together now: Inhale. Exhale. Better! These seemingly insubstantial drip drip-drips, are nature's "first milk", called colostrum, and are *hugely* important to baby. Nothing else on Earth provides as much densely packed, immune-boosting nutrition. Worth the effort, moms! Feeling better, LCs?)

As foretold by my sister, Ashley, the day my milk truly "came in" after having Clark was somewhat of an emotional rollercoaster sort of day. If you haven't been there yourself yet, guys, the hormones are just shy of palpable. Imagine going to bed one evening looking rather like Olive Oyl up top only to wake up (as if I slept... ha!) the next morning looking more like Pamela Anderson. I remember Alicia, my oldest sister, coming over that morning to help with some housework, glancing at my impossible-not-to-see boobs, and saying "Wow, Whit! I didn't know they had it in them. That's impressive!" You see, everyone, in addition to the short nipples God blessed me with, He also built me with bitty boobies. Just a few weeks ago, I finally caved to the reality that I am unable to fit into any normal woman-sized bra, so I, as a 31-year-old, bought a handful of 'bralettes' from the junior's section. How did the Boob Quip Queen, AKA Alicia, respond when she found out about my purchase?

- "At least Syd and Lilly [her daughters] will have someone with experience to refer to when they need training bras in a couple of years!"

Ha. Ha. Ha. Well the day my milk came in, anyway, I had far more goods up North than I ever needed or desired.

I've been trying to think of a good comparison for those of you who have never or will never experience engorgement firsthand. The best analogy I've got is a bee sting. Have you ever been stung by a bee and experienced the warm, rock-hard, tender swelling that comes with it? OK—now picture that being your chest… times two. Breasts engorged with milk look and feel a little like massive bee stings—swollen, tight-as-all-get-out, and sore.

So your milk has come in, you're now experiencing a true "let down"— a weird, almost electric (sometimes uncomfortable, actually) feeling as the process of milk release starts with each feeding— and baby is finally receiving more than a single drop of fluid every few hours. The sun is shining, the birds are singings, and all is (hardly) well in the world… when suddenly you feel like you're going into labor again while feeding your cherub. What the heck?! As we've already established, the havoc wreaked on a woman's body both during and after pregnancy is a very real thing. Because the uterus has been so well used and abused following delivery, the body has to work to return it to its original shape. How is this achieved? More *contractions*. Remember those blasted uterus checks? Well, besides the manual stimulation of a nurse's hands, there is something else capable of signaling the uterus to contract yet again: hormones. And what stimulates hormone release? Oh, right! Breastfeeding.

To any pregnant reader out there who may not have already known about this weird phenomenon… sorry in advance! Although these contractions are *nothing* compared to those endured during the actual process of delivery, they were enough to make me cringe and, quite frankly, get a little sassy with The Guy Upstairs. I understand that getting in shape isn't usually an easy, comfortable change… I mean I'm pretty sure most swimsuit models don't earn their bods by sitting on the couch in their cozies… so I shouldn't have been taken aback when a notable-amount-of-ouch was required for my womb to reshape itself. Seriously, though? I felt like God was duping me. After you've endured the *super*-significant-amount-of-ouch that coincides with labor and delivery, there is no such thing as welcome pain in your lady regions. Even *thinking* about a menstrual cramp those first days after delivery was enough to give me anxiety.

Sadly, both your lower *and* upper regions will be sore and recovering when you make it home from the hospital. Even with the use of a shield for Clark, my nipples were crazy, crazy tender those first days. I literally squinted one eye and contorted my face in anticipation of his mouth coming into contact with my girls. My buttons both looked and felt pretty darn awful in the beginning. Oh, and Annie? Well the mere fact that she attempted to latch onto my bare skin at all was a miracle to me, leading me to make the mistake of allowing her to grab on there in *any* fashion in the beginning. Are you curious how that one turned out? Well, instead of me heeding the advice to remove her from the breast and start afresh whenever the latch didn't feel "right", as any and every lactation consultant will tell you, I gave a super-premature "WOO HOO!" if and when Annie latched to *any* degree. I practically had to hold my breath because of how uncomfortable I was during feedings, and once, I even experienced the joy of Annie literally tearing the skin around my nipple. Her mouth was full of blood, resulting in me jokingly referring to her as my "little cannibal" for a few days. Strawberry smoothie, anyone? Ha. Sorry. But seriously, guys, who tells you about this stuff? It happens!

You know what people *do* tell you? That breastfeeding is *simpler* and more convenient than formula feeding. The line of thinking here is this: While your boobs go everywhere with you without choice, bottle feeding supplies don't. I'll give it to you that formula feeding a baby may require a lot of stuff, like purified water, a can of formula, a bottle, and, perhaps, a bottle warmer, but breastfeeding, folks? It's *just* as complicated those first days. Before the LCs out there pull out their matches again and burn me at the stake… YES, <u>after</u> the routine of breastfeeding is established and both mom and baby learn the process, it *is* beautiful, and precious, and so, so, so, so much simpler than bottle feeding or pumping (though still a commitment and sacrifice for momma!). Until you get to that point, though, which never happened for me with Clark and took like a good two months with Annie? Not. Simple. Two basic requirements, right? Boob and baby? How about the nipple shield we've already discussed? How about nipple *cream* for preventing and treating tenderness? How about the bulky-but-totally-essential nursing pillow for better positioning? How about a breast milk collector for those of us who leak from the non-feeding side? How about nursing pads to keep our clothing dry for those times we spot a baby in Target and start jetting milk from our geysers like Old Faithful (yep, happened!)? Oh, and how about our old pal, the breast pump, and all of its pipes, pieces, and plugs? *This* is real life.

A few lines back, I divulged the reality of breastfeeding Clark. It never worked. Could I have made it happen, or could I have pushed myself or my guy just a little further? Yes, I'm sure. For us, however, for lots of reasons, traditional breastfeeding just never happened. After we were discharged from the hospital, I continued the feeding process I was taught, including the use of our trusty nipple shield and pump. Because breastfeeding never came to Clark or myself as second nature in the hospital, it was recommended that we follow up with a lactation consultant following discharge. We did this on more than one occasion.

Jonathan and I spent lots of time showing the lactation consultant what our routine looked like, how I was positioning Clark during feedings, and sharing our concerns. She watched, assisted, provided wisdom and insight from her *years* of experience, and ultimately said to me after our second or third appointment… "Clark is just a strange feeder!" Ha! Hilarious, and true, but not exactly reassuring when coming from an expert on the subject. Because I totally, one-million-percent agreed and was so beyond frustrated that fifteen minutes or more of feeding my baby was giving him an intake of like a whopping four *milliliters* of breastmilk (what the heck, kiddo??), I asked her if foregoing the baby-to-breast concept in order to elect pumping exclusively was an option. Her reply?

- "Breast milk is the key. It doesn't matter where it comes from."

Even though she was quick with her response, our lactation consultant wasn't unrealistic and just-as-quickly explained that pumping long-term was a mammoth commitment, one that most moms (especially working moms) could not sustain. Although I didn't understand the enormity of the decision I was making… challenge accepted!

Who doesn't love a good challenge, right? Well, on this one, me apparently. This challenge, I anything-but-loved. Since I'm all about painting honest and accurate pictures for you, here's one: pumping *sucks*. It sucks so much, in fact, that it creates this almost camaraderie-like connection among its performers. You can be sitting at a sales presentation with a complete stranger, for example, somehow get onto the topic of newborns, discover that you share the bond of pumping… and suddenly, you are friends for life. I kid you not, this real-life happened to me—just last night, in fact.

Jonathan and I are in the process of purchasing new windows for our home[3] and signed a contract with a local glass company at our dining room table last evening. The young professional who sold us the windows was very patient and understanding as our three-year-old dictator shouted commands from the kitchen, where he was playing in the sink, and our one-year-old dictator demanded more cookies. He smiled through it all and then shared that he and his wife welcomed a little one into the world only three months ago.

We chatted a bit about the "glories" of sleep deprivation and how having a second child seems like such an improbability in those early, hard days. Then, the topic of breastfeeding came up, and this gentleman shared that his wife is a pumper. An *exclusive* pumper. Naturally, as soon as my ears caught wind of these words, a whole new, figurative "window" was opened (I'm dying over here at my lame-o connection between our window purchase and my illustration, by the way. I think I need to get out a bit more than I do. Ha! Sorry…) We vented, and chatted, and laughed, and complained for several minutes about the experience that is pumping. By the end of our conversation, I was offering my own contact information to someone I'd never even met simply because she and I were, and are, fellow soldiers now.

While I don't regret for a single second doing what I did for my child, I'll be the first one to tell you that this was the most monumental commitment I have ever made in my life. I'm not kidding. I think I actually told my husband once that I deserved a sizable gift for the sacrifices I made during Clark's first year of life in order to keep the rivers flowin' (and by the way, love, I don't recall ever having received one… hint, hint). I mean, I semi-considered hosting a pump-burning party when these puppies finally closed up shop. Despite the one super-cool thing about making milk like Henrietta Holstein, which is that I was literally eating 3500 to 4000 calories a day without gaining an ounce[4], here is a list of sometimes comical, always sucky, pumping realities I faced:

- For four months, I pumped six times daily for 15 minutes each session. For an additional five months, I pumped five times daily. Without the added (gobs of) time for setup, cleanup, and the dreaded washing of pump parts (it's the *worst*...Amen, pumpers?), it is fair to say that I spent over 22,000 minutes (that's over 350 hours!) pumping. Awful.

- Once, after falling asleep on the couch with my hubby while binge-watching some *Downton Abbey*, I woke in a state of delirium and literally *cried* because I had to pump before going to bed. I'm pretty sure Jonathan actually hooked me up to the sucker while I threw my giant, toddler fit and repeatedly whined "I don't want to do it! I don't want to do it!" I am so, super mature, in case you can't tell.

- Because I didn't want to risk reducing my supply[5], I got up at 3AM to pump until Clark was about four months old... even after he started sleeping through the night at around nine weeks old (don't gag, parent readers, Annie didn't sleep through the night until she was like nine *months* old—she may have been easier than her brother in many ways, but not on this one!). It took me getting sick repeatedly from a lack of sleep and a weakened immune system to finally cave and sleep the whole night through without waking to pump.

- For almost an entire school year, I pumped twice a day, every day at work (in, essentially, a closet, by the way). In addition to the personal stress this caused *me*, it was also a hardship for my coworkers as I am a school nurse and was the only medically-trained employee in the building the vast majority of the time. My right to pump was, in fact, once a staff meeting bullet point. Embarrassing, to say the least!

- In order to ensure that The Twin Peaks wouldn't be too full and cause me discomfort, I once pumped in the car (car adapter for the win!) on my way to a 10K race that my friend, Sue, and I were participating in. She called me nuts the whole way. I'd like to point out that I ran like the wind that day. I think it was the crazy-fast, lactation-induced metabolism I had going for me.

- Pumping at home is bad enough, but pumping anywhere else? It just plain stinks. I can't even tell you the number of times I either forgot ice packs or lids, so the fruits of my labor were painstakingly poured down the drain or out the car window. All pumpers know that whoever coined the phrase "don't cry over spilt milk" sure as shoot wasn't a lactating mother. Why bother if you don't have the supplies you need, one may ask? Well, skip a pumping *ever*, and you risk lowering your supply or having to carry around merciless melons.

- While sometimes possible, planning around events when it comes to pumping isn't always a feasible task. There are two specific occasions that come to mind when I recollect on this thought. First, I can remember being at my sister's house for a several-hour-long birthday party for one of her (thousand) sons. Because I had no choice but to pump, I sat isolated in a room by myself for almost a half hour while the party carried on without me. I felt like I was in timeout, honestly. Second, when Jonathan and I once hosted our annual Friends-mas (a Christmas celebration amongst friends, of course), I didn't want to miss out on the fun and excitement. Solution? I stood behind the pony wall separating our kitchen and family room and exposed myself from the shoulders up only while I pumped away[6]. Bryan, my best friend Kelly's husband, is practically allergic to the sight, thought, and/or discussion of any bodily fluid (or cream-based food... love you, Bry!), so, obviously, this was exactly how he had hoped to spend his evening.

As you can tell, pumping and I have a reputation. When Annie came to town, I resolved that I was *not* going the route of the pump. Don't get me wrong, I would have at least tried it again if I didn't have another choice, but I was determined to breastfeed in a traditional sense the second time around. There were—no surprise—many reasons why I felt this way. Do you want to know the one that topped the list, though? Because I had a crazy-as-they-come, twenty-month-old toddler who other, more polite folks called (still do, in fact) "active" or "busy". I could clearly picture Clark climbing on my head, falling down the stairs (again), or drinking out of the toilet while I was tethered to an electrical socket for another million hours of my life for months on end. No, thanks!

I was *so* resolved not to become dependent, once again, on the breast pump that I actually did myself more harm than good in the beginning with Annie. Remember my short nipples? Well, they didn't go anywhere or miraculously gain length from Baby One to Baby Two. While I put Annie *immediately* to my boob when she was born, kept her there as long as she wanted to be there regardless of visitors, and found that she definitely had more interest than her brother from the start, latching still wasn't easy or perfect. This wasn't a huge deal in the hospital when I was only making teeny-tiny amounts of milk, but when the floodgates opened at home, I got *swollen*. Take a guess at what happens to short nipples when they are attached to a swollen boob? They get shorter!

I can remember being so tight, so sore, and so so so frustrated one evening when Annie couldn't latch. I called Ashley, apparently my first line, "save me!" contact when it came to babies, and cried. I simply didn't know what else to do. Here's how that phone conversation went:

ASH (*composed, stating the obvious*): Just *pump* a few minutes to relieve the pressure, and then pop her on there!

ME (anything but composed, more closely resembling a whiny, mopey toddler): I. Don't. Want. To. Pump. Again.

It took far more convincing than it should have for my sister to assure me that aiding myself a little bit here and again with my mortal enemy didn't mean that I would be tied to it forever. When I relented? Winner, winner, breastmilk dinner... for Annie, of course.

In terms of breastfeeding and pumping, I've got a lot of complaints. There's no denying that, and I think I've made it plainly clear. Truthfully though, what I gained with each of my children through these experiences was worth every bit of the effort I put in. In pumping (and pumping, and pumping) for Clark, I learned that I was willing to sacrifice a *lot* of time and a *lot* of convenience to do what I felt was best for my child. In overcoming obstacles with Annie so that I could breastfeed her traditionally, I learned that there is another side to the breastfeeding mountain I simply hadn't made it to with Clark. After the struggle and after the learning, breastfeeding really *is* totally the opposite of gross and (dare I say it...) *easy*. Some of my fondest, most-cherished moments with Annie as an infant, in fact, are the times she and I spent together while breastfeeding. Especially because I had another, still-super-dependent toddler to take care of, I looked forward to "our time". Even at 3AM. Here's something crazy for you. Something that I never, ever would have said when I was in the thick of the newborn days. In terms of feeding my little ones: very, very occasionally, I miss it *all*.

Regardless of where you find (or found) yourself on the breastfeeding spectrum, let's resolve to remove the shame associated with feeding our babies in any form. Do what you do because you love your child, period. Want to feed your babe formula so that the hubs can help out and you can be a little better rested and in-tune to baby during the day? Good for you! Want to breastfeed even though you're working full time? Get it, girl! Want to consider bottles because you've given breastfeeding your best shot and it's just not what you thought it would be? Hold your head high! Babies need nutrition to thrive, and guess what, guys? Hate away, haters, but solid nutrition can come from a boob OR a bottle. No matter which route you choose or are forced onto, believe me when I say that you will experience lots and lots and lots of tears (chapter five, here we come!) coupled with lots of joy.

---

1. Want the truth? I had one foot in the "gross" camp before gazing into the eyes of my own babies.
2. Waking a baby and/or keeping a baby awake is like the worst kind of irony... *especially* at night time when you'd sell a kidney for a few hours of sleep. Seriously.
3. Barf, by the way. If I'm going to fork out over 10 grand on a home improvement project, it would be a whole lot cooler if I could score a shiny, new bathroom with a jetted tub or something in the end. Windows? Boring!
4. Funny story: Once, my mom came and stayed the night with Clark and I while Jonathan was away on business. After Clark was in bed for the evening, I sat down on the couch with half of the refrigerator and gorged blissfully while watching *Downton Abbey* (apparently good boob stories and *Downton* just go together...). Mom sat there and stared at me in amazement. I don't think she's ever seen a person eat so much food in one sitting, especially since my sisters and I have always jokingly referred to her as a mouse because of the three bites of anything it takes to fill her up. Mouse is to Mom as python... you know, the snakes that eat elephants basically... is to Whitney.

5.   Anyone who knows anything about my pumping journey will laugh heartily at this… I may wear bralettes, guys, but I produced over a half-gallon a day, had a frozen stash enough to last Clark until his second birthday, and donated *thousands* of ounces of excess. Heck, I even sold a few thousand ounces for medical research. I was a milk-producing machine/freak.

6.   I'm also fairly certain I made that same crew take an intermission during the movie *Interstellar*[7] for a pump break on another occasion. No biggie! If you haven't seen it, you'll need like *six* intermissions just to keep your brain from imploding. So mind-bending, yet so good!

7.   Is it even legal to make a reference inside of a reference? Who knows, but I'm about to do it…
      Interstellar. Directed by Christopher Nolan, Paramount Pictures, 2014.

5 CRYING UPON CRYING UPON CRYING

Let it be known that I am not much of a crier. Releasing my emotions, in the form of tears anyway, simply isn't that commonplace for me. While I know that there are men out there who cry just as much, if not more, than most women[1], I am comparing myself to others of my gender when I say this. To be sure that I am assessing myself fairly, I asked Jonathan the following question just now:

- "On a scale of one to ten, in terms of *women*, how often do I cry with a one being 'never' and a ten being 'always'".

His very quick response?

- "Maybe a two or three."

Case in point.

Part of this, I believe, is in my upbringing. For starters, my mom is super pragmatic. Don't get me wrong, it's one of the qualities I love about her, but if I call or text Mom in the middle of what I deem a crisis, her responses are always practical, not emotional. If I'm being honest, she doesn't usually say what I *want* her to say... you know, things like:

- "You're totally right. Follow your heart. Everything will be ok!"

... she says what is *best*... something more like:

- "You have an awesome job with amazing benefits. You'd be silly to leave it."

In case you're curious on the *when* and *why* my mom may have said something like this to me, well, here comes a long, but pertinent, story...

After I had Clark, I returned to full-time work not because I wanted to, but because Jonathan and I weren't in a financial place where another option existed. When I found out that I was pregnant with Annie, there was an evening early on during which I poured out my heart to my hubby. I explained that I just *couldn't* handle returning to work full-time after bringing a child into the world again. I longed (and felt very called) to be at home. Being the support that he is, Jonathan took this to prayer and immediately started looking for new employment. To make a long story short, God provided a perfect job for him, and I informed my employer both that I was pregnant and that I would not be returning to work full-time.

Because I worked as a certified school nurse on a professional contract exactly like the classroom teachers surrounding me (who basically ALL worked full-time), I didn't expect a part-time offer... but that's exactly what I received. Any and *every* request that I laid before the school district I was working for was granted. Although my true hope was to stay at home for good, I felt obligated (if I'm being honest) to work in this new capacity since my employer was being so accommodating of my needs.

From the sixth through thirteenth months of Annie's life, I worked two days weekly while she and Clark were cared for by my sister Ashley. Add to the reality that this was a set schedule with great hours and phenomenal pay year-round despite the fact that I had the summer months off... and it was about the cushiest, cake-iest setup a working mom could ask for. You know what, though? None of that mattered. I still wanted *badly* to be at home. More than money, Jonathan wanted me to find fulfillment, peace, and happiness in what I was doing, and he could sense that bringing in a paycheck just wasn't doing that for me any longer. At that point, we decided that I would stay at home full-time.

When I finally took the news of our decision to my mom (I avoided the conversation for as long as possible because I *knew* what she was going to say… maturity at its finest! I told you, guys, I'm the mature-est…) and got the response I got, she wasn't being an unfeeling, heartless jerk. She was being reasonable and rational, *especially* given her past. Without turning this tangent into an entire chapter itself, my mom endured a long, long marriage in which she never experienced support, encouragement, or healthy love. Instead, she worked hard to provide for herself, her (undeserving, yet receiving) spouse, and her three children.

It's this history, I believe, that creates my mom's pragmatism… and understandably so. She is the first one to admit that she wants what is best for my sisters and I in every situation, *always*, even if it means saying some harsh or honest things. What it all boils down to is that she wants us to be able to stand on our own two feet and support ourselves like she had to. She's my hero, and although I may not always like what she has to say, I give her full permission to tell me like it is every day. She's earned that right. I share this story and background with you so that you understand the following: While my mom is definitely one to support the dreams of my sisters and I and one that always trusts and *eventually* supports our decisions, she's not one to side with us on all things simply because we are her daughters. Pretty cool, actually.

I saw my mom cry at times growing up, but her tears were always warranted and purposeful, it seemed. Mom's tears were, and still are, reserved for "big" moments[2]… things like births, deaths, diagnoses, weddings, graduations, and chick flicks. How'd you like that subtle placement? Beyond my mom, my extended family, as a whole, just isn't an overly emotional, touchy-feely kind of crew. Yes, of course, I've shared *occasional* tears with my cousins, aunts, and uncles, but we are much more likely to be found stuffing our faces or belly-laughing over whatever game Ashley is forcing upon my stoic Uncle Spark.

When I started dating Jonathan and was introduced to his extended family, I'm fairly certain I hugged more during the *first* encounter with them than I had in my entire life. Here's an example. I have been babysitting my niece, Madison, up to four days a week for over nine months now. On each and every one of these days, I have received a hug and a "Have a great day!" (super genuine, by the way) from my brother-in-law, Justin. Jonathan's family, on both sides, is comprised of lots of super-sweet, super-feeling people. Many of them cry...bunches.

Whatever the reason may be, I am not one to vent my feelings through tears. Pent up anger? Oh, yeah. Stuffing my mouth with chocolate? You betcha! (I am very literally eating a double chocolate cookie topped with chocolate frosting as I type this. In case you were wondering, it's *delicious*). When I'm PMSing, you'd be a lot more likely to find me with my face in a peanut butter jar or with a murder weapon in my hand ([half] kidding!) than blotting away tears with a tissue. I'm not a robot or anything, mind you. A few times a year, I'll have an ugly cry at church when I am feeling particularly struck by the music or the message, at home when I am feeling burnt out in caring for two (or three, when I'm babysitting) tiny tyrants, or in my car on one of the infrequent occasions I find myself alone and able to let go of all of the cares in the world.

Following the births of both Clark and Annie, though? Holy, holiest of craps. I cried. And I cried. And I cried. And then I cried again. The days in the hospital weren't *so* bad, as far as tears go, I think mostly because there was a constant barrage of visitors, and I was still a little shell-shocked with, well, *everything*. As soon as we returned home, however, it was almost as if someone opened the floodgates. The first night, as you may recall, I shed puddles of frantic tears when Clark choked on his own spit up after a 3AM feeding. Because, until this point in my life, having a "good cry" triggered some sort of internal register and reset the counter for another month, or two...or six... I awoke the next morning looking completely-awful but hopeful that better, tear-free days were ahead. Wishful thinking!

Ashley basically told me that I would feel like a lunatic the day my milk came in, and that "special" day just so happened to be the day following Clark's choking fiasco. *Any*thing, and *every*thing brought me to uncontrollable, ugly sob-fests that day. The best example of this was when Mom and Alicia came to help Jonathan and I with some housework. Clark was comfortable and completely asleep in his Pack 'N Play while the hubs and I were looking *bad* on the couch. My mom took pity on our tired, wrecked souls and said "Why don't you go lay down upstairs and get some rest while Clark sleeps?" She could sense my hesitancy as a new, I-have-no-clue-what-I'm-doing, mom and added... "I promise that if he wakes up, I'll come get you."

I heaved a huge sigh, relented to my fatigue, and dragged myself up the stairs with Jonathan following closely behind. While laying down in our bed certainly felt *good*, I was hit within seconds by an almost tangible surge of emotion. I felt like I was sitting on the beach with my eyes fixed on the ocean as a tsunami approached. The tears were coming (again!), and nothing was going to stop them. Jonathan and I were facing opposite of one another, and because I wanted *so* much to let him get the rest we badly needed, I attempted to cry in silence. My tears may have fallen without sound, but my shoulders trembled with such violence that I actually shook the bed. Jonathan turned to me quickly and asked, "Are you crying? What's wrong?" In the moments following those two simple questions, I wept like I had *never* before wept in my life. My cries were guttural. Between the sobs, I tried my best to form words and, eventually, managed to convey to my husband that Clark was simply "too far away".

My guy may have only been a few dozen feet from me, but it was the first time since his birth that he was out of my sight other than for medical care. After carrying Clark in the depths of my core for *months*... after nourishing him, and growing him, and *feeling* him... it was the first moment I realized that he and I weren't physically connected anymore and that I couldn't protect him or shield him from the dangers and hurts of the world. Big thoughts to stem from such a silly situation, I know, but oh, how my heart hurt in that instant. Knowing that we weren't about to achieve any semblance of "rest" as things stood, Jonathan asked if I wanted to head back downstairs.... and down we went. My mom chuckled when she saw us coming, almost as if she expected our premature return, and she moved her cleaning efforts elsewhere so that I could cry myself to sleep on the couch. Right next to Clark. Where I needed to be.

When Ashley saw me later that evening with my swollen eyes and blotchy face, I think she was taken aback for just a brief second by my ultra-raw-hideousness before her own post-natal memories came flooding back. I'll never forget the look of empathy and I've-totally-been-there on her face when she said to me, "Oh sissy! It gets better!!!". Four (crazy woman) times before, she *had* stood where I stood. Just like me, she had done the hard work of carrying and delivering her babes and was thrown headfirst into a realm of sleeplessness and hormonal shifts unlike *anything* imaginable.

Having a baby is seriously the craziest thing ever. It's kind of like this: Here's a new full-time job (I mean full-time, full-time... like 24/7), a new family, a new (nonexistent) sleep pattern, a new (nonexistent) routine, a new (dripping) body... Oh! And all of those hormones you've grown accustomed to for nearly a year now? BLAMMO. Gone. No wonder I cried. No wonder *you* cried, moms! No wonder you *will* cry, preggos!

Crying, in the beginning, will become almost so second nature that it'll just feel like a part of your day. This was true for me for like a solid two weeks after the births of both Clark and Annie. Because those puffy-eyed, drippy-nosed days were forever branded in the back of my mind after having Clark, I even made a *game* out of my crying when Annie came to town. Jonathan and I actually took bets on how many subsequent days I would cry after her delivery. Every morning when we "woke up"[3], we would look at each other and say whether or not we thought that day would be *the* day when I'd make it to sundown without waterworks. I'm pretty sure I thought I'd get myself together the second time around a lot sooner than I actually did. I'm also pretty sure Jonathan had me pegged to cry every day for like a month. (He wasn't too far off, either!) Regardless of who did or didn't "win" our little game, I cried for every reason from A to Z in the postpartum days. Pregnant? You will too! I can almost promise it.

- You will cry in frustration.

    Remember my Annie-can't-latch tears? The tears I cried because I wanted nothing more than to nourish my child with the milk my body was surely producing but unable to release? *Pure* frustration! Becoming a parent, even the second or *seventh* time around, is all about change that often times doesn't come easily. There will be lots of big and little things, especially in the beginning, that are frustrating enough to bring you to tears. Maybe it's getting your little one to eat. Maybe it's getting your little one to sleep. Maybe it's trying to find time to shower... ever.

- You will cry in love.

    After we brought Annie home, I'll never forget waking that first morning as a family of four and just *sobbing* to Jonathan about how much I <u>loved</u> my children. In my opinion, there is not a more concrete love than the love felt by a parent for his or her newborn child. It's such an overwhelming love, to be honest, that it almost physically causes distress. My ridiculous outburst when I attempted to nap one floor above a sleeping, infant Clark, for example? The pangs of love.

- You will cry in fatigue.

    No matter how hard I try to paint an accurate picture of *just how tiring* it is to be a new parent, until you've experienced it yourself, I will never be able to do it justice. I'm not sure what it was, in particular, about this one night after bringing Clark home that caused such a meltdown on my part, but I never before (and never since, actually) felt quite so physically and mentally depleted in all of my life. Because I was just, well, s p e n t, these recollections are a bit of a blur... but I can remember waking up to Clark's cries for the second or third time in only a handful of hours and *losing* it. I curled up in the fetal position, started crying myself, and repeated time and time again "I can't do it... I can't do it... I can't do it...". Jonathan woke to my completely self centered, mess-of-a-moment, changed Clark, brought him to me (we were still attempting breast feeding at the time), and tried his best to motivate me with words that were loving, yet kind of terse, at the same time: "You *can* do this, Girl. You *have* to do this. *We* have to do this." I won't lie to you and say that my attitude was suddenly one of bliss or that I fed my baby with a joyful heart in that moment, but I survived, and I appreciated the sturdy support of my husband.

- You will cry in longing.

    Perhaps the ugliest and real-est tears of them all were the tears I cried over a life that was lost. *My* life... before baby (or babies). I've said it lots of times already, and I'll say it again, but I LOVED my children tremendously from their first breath. *That* was never up for debate. What *was* up for debate, however, was how much I "loved" losing all sense of normalcy. With Clark, I missed sleep. I missed being able to feed my own face without worrying about whether or not someone else's needed to be fed first. I missed routine. I missed time with my husband that didn't revolve around a third party. I missed feeling as though I had any sense of ownership over my own body instead of functioning merely as a milk factory. I missed being able to leave the house *when* I wanted, to go *where* I wanted, without having to think about the approximately 6,642 things I would have to bring along... including a baby who was never, ever a good car rider like everyone assured Jonathan and I he would be. With Annie, I missed a nap schedule. I missed one-on-one time with Clark. I missed the little bit of sleep I actually started getting again. I missed Daddy being able to help with feedings. Oh, and of course I missed being able to leave the house *when* I wanted, to go *where* I wanted, without having to think about the approximately 6,64**3** things I would now have to bring along... including a baby AND a toddler who were never, ever good car riders like everyone assured Jonathan and I they would be.

- You will cry in loneliness.

    We've already established that having a baby is quite a paradoxical experience. It can be the absolute best and absolute worst all at the same time. Another strange paradox of parenthood is the sense of simultaneous community and isolation that it brings to moms and dads. On one hand, having a baby makes you closer with others because it helps you understand and relate better to parents, parent siblings, and parent friends. It sort of brings things "full circle". Until *I* was a mom, I couldn't possibly comprehend the full effect of the sacrifices my own mom made for my sisters and me when we were growing up. And when I *did* become a mom? Well, it was absolutely bananas to me that my mom had lived (and survived) the journey not once, or twice, but *three* times around. Because of how demanding an experience it is, parenthood also kind of forces you to accept the help of others (when it is offered and available) in the form of food prep, help with housework, and help with childcare (if you aren't a first-timer). On the other hand, though, having a baby can make you feel so very alone. For starters, it's just *hard* to get out of the house when a baby comes to town. Even seemingly menial tasks like picking up a handful of groceries becomes something that requires loads of planning and a complete assessment of risk versus reward. Then, there's the feeling like you're the only person on the planet who is so tired and so out-of-touch with the outside world. Attending events of any sort for the first month or so? Hard, hard. You've got to plan ahead for feedings, bring a giant bottle of hand sanitizer for all of the touchy-feelies in the crowd, and prepare yourself mentally to look and act like you have some semblance of an idea of what you're doing. Being around friends and family is stressful enough, but anywhere with crowds (church, for example) in the beginning? Might as well forget about it if you're a germaphobe and a please-don't-touch-my-baby-unless-you-actually-*know*-me kind of person like I am.

- You will cry in the-opposite-of-loneliness.

    Sometimes, the sense of community that comes along with having a baby is totally great. Sometimes, not so much. In the next chapter, we'll dig deep into the concept of visitors as I relive and recount my stories as they relate to guests in the initial postnatal days. Did I ever cry in the presence of visitors? You betcha! Family members and friends are almost always well-meaning, but sometimes also super-duper *overwhelming*.

- You will cry in envy.

    Before I say anything further, please know that my husband is beyond amazing and sincerely *wanted* to help with our babies, from day one, in any way fathomable. Because we bottle-fed breastmilk to Clark, Jonathan often assisted with overnight feedings while I pumped. Further, since Clark basically required a song and dance to be put back to sleep...always... Jonathan definitely had his share of late-night and/or early-morning "quality time" with our guy. Annie, however, was different. Unlike her brother, she didn't want a bottle, nor did Momma want to pump (especially not overnight!). Further, she just wasn't as "needy" overnight as her brother had been. She was awake *often* and for *a while*, don't get me wrong, but after she latched and ate (which did sometimes take 45 or more minutes in the beginning) I could basically plop her down and call it a "win". End result? Although appreciated, Jonathan wasn't really *needed*, per se, at night with Annie. This is especially true due to the reality that my husband is not a fast waker. If I have an alarm set on my phone, it sounds, I turn it off, and I'm out of bed. Jonathan's alarm? Well, it sounds, and sounds, and sounds, I reach over and smack or shake him, he snoozes it, and we repeat the process again in nine minutes... times like three. Jonathan offered time and time again to get up when Annie needed to eat overnight so that he could change her diaper before and after, as needed. In order for this to happen, however, I would have to wake him first and allow a few moments for his brain to even acknowledge my existence and process my request. Then, it would take him five or more minutes just to get up and get moving before even addressing her diaper. By the time Jonathan was handing over a dried Annie, I could've had her changed, latched, and filling her belly had I simply done it myself (Sorry, love! You know it's true...). Although placing more on my own plate, it was easier for me to just handle the overnight business alone. I'll never forget the first time that Jonathan was asleep soundly enough the entire night through that he didn't hear any of the waking/changing/feeding happenings. When he rubbed his eyes the next morning just before 6AM, opened them far enough to see me feeding Annie at the bedside and said something akin to, "Wow! I can't believe this is the first time she woke to eat all night!", I wanted to smack the crap out of him right then and there. That day, and many other days if I'm being honest, my friends, I cried tears of envy. Being a parent is super hard, period, but in those moments of wanting nothing more than a solid night of sleep for *myself*, being a breastfeeding mom was super, <u>super</u> hard.

- You will cry in wonder.

   You just created a life. Think about that. You. Just. Created. A. *Life*. Nuts! I can remember *so* many tears for both Clark and Annie that originated in thoughts of how miraculous and amazing their little lives were to me. I couldn't help but thank God for choosing me to be their Mommy and for blessing me with the opportunity to aid in their growth and prosperity. I enjoy a good challenge and am an accomplishment-oriented individual. Being given the gift of parenthood, some days, kind of felt like the biggest and best opportunity ever... enough to bring me to tears.

- You will cry in fear.

  One morning, well into our "game" of For How Many Consecutive Days Will Whitney Lose It, I said to Jonathan, with confidence, "I can feel it! Today's going to be the first day without tears." Not long after making this bold statement, Jonathan took Clark outside to play in the front yard while I fed Annie. True to form, Annie pooped as she ate because classy just runs in our family. I wrapped things up (in more than one way...), laid Annie down, and started changing her, as always. When I opened the diaper, however, the nurse in me panicked. What did I discover? Blood. A non-medical parent may have missed it in all actuality as it wasn't like her poo was bright red or anything. It was black-ish and looked like a bunch of coffee grounds. Coffee grounds in the toilet or in a diaper, non-nurses, is no good. Coffee grounds=digested blood. As a medical professional, I stayed calm, phoned the doctor, and rationally signaled to Jonathan that I needed his attention. Oh, hardly! I started bawling like a nutter, somehow blubbered enough sensible words to the secretary at our pediatrician's office to secure an appointment, and then called Jonathan in hysterics on his cell phone even though I could see him from the window[4]. Wanna know what I real-life said to him before I even mentioned Annie? "Well, it looks like I'm going to cry today!" Ha! As a parent, there is nothing more sacred than the health and safety of your children. When either of those things are in jeopardy, there is an internal cord that is struck hard, and it will shake you to the core. In that moment, I was unable to think rationally or slow my racing brain. My mind was flooded with fear. Fear that Annie was allergic to my breastmilk. Fear that something, perhaps, was *wrong* with my baby girl[5].

- You will cry in, well, who knows what!

> Possibly my favorite crying story of all when it comes to the births of my children occurred one evening as Jonathan and I sat down to eat dinner. Clark was sleeping peacefully in his Rock 'n Play and our food was fully-prepped and ready-to-go thanks to some kind soul from church. Because we were (and still are) beyond sophisticated, the hubs and I set up our TV trays in front of the tube and started to dig in off of paper plates. For no good reason at all, I just started *sobbing*. The best part was that when Jonathan looked over at me and saw me in pieces for the 100th time in a handful of days, it didn't even phase him. He shoveled another bite into his mouth and gave me a sincere, yet here-we-go-again "You OK?". My response was, "I don't even know why I'm crying!", and I didn't. For whatever reason, I just needed the emotional release, so I ate my meal while both laughing and crying at my insanity[6].

Remember my friend Stacy, with whom I shared an honest "pep talk" a few weeks prior to her son's arrival—the spark that sort of lit the fire for compiling and sharing this entire collection of thoughts and memories? Well, she and I sat down for coffee together when our babies were a few months old and life had "normalized" a bit. With our cherubs in the care of their capable and supportive daddies, it was nice to connect in person, mom to mom, and sort of celebrate the reality that we had survived the toughest, longest, darkest parts of newborn life. We had a chance to really discuss these wonderful, yet *terrible*, first days... together. Just like me, Stacy confessed that she cried in the beginning, all the time.

Becoming a parent, in so many ways, feels like taking your comfortable, predictable, sleep-filled life and standing it on its head. Your body is essentially wounded and attempting recovery in the exact *opposite* of ideal conditions, hormones are running amok, and everything is different. If you are pregnant, stock up on tissues... now. Seriously! Want to hear the cool part, though, guys? It all comes full circle. I may have cried in fatigue, and frustration, and envy, and loneliness in those early days, but I also cried bittersweet tears of *remembrance* when this part of my life came to an end.

Almost a year ago now, my hubby and I made the decision that our family was complete. To solidify and finalize this choice, we took surgical steps in the form of a few "snip, snip, snips"... if you know what I mean. As Jonathan and I sat together in the waiting room prior to his procedure, we were surprised to find ourselves both in tears. Believe me when I say that there was no sense of cold feet or regret—no matter how much we love our children we knew that we were doner-than-done with two—but there was a sense of mourning that we both felt and acknowledged in that a beautiful and wonderful phase of our lives was coming to a close. Never again would new life be brought into our home and into our family, and that was a lot for the two of us to process. The journey of parenthood is the hardest thing ever, that is the absolute truth. Thankfully, though, it's not the only truth. The journey of parenthood is also the most special thing ever.

Post Script:

I started this chapter by saying "Let it be known that I am not much of a crier." Well, everyone, let it *also* be known that, apparently, making such a statement publicly makes God giggle. Since I started writing *Crying Upon Crying Upon Crying* a week or so ago, I have cried an uncharacteristic amount. It's laughable. For starters, my BFF, Kelly, shared some super-fun news that turned me into an instant fountain of tears. She's pregnant and expecting her first little one in the Fall! Welcome to the simultaneous joy and misery, Kell!

On top of this excitement, it's New Year's Day, I've got a bit of the blues which always greet me at the end of another holiday season, I'm menstrual, Annie has been sick and either barfing, pooping, coughing, or wheezing for almost a solid three weeks now (which equals little sleep for Mommy and Daddy), and the recent single digit temperatures have kept a certain toddler boy (who *thrives* on fresh air) cooped up inside. At my family's New Year's Eve celebration last evening, Jonathan and I left just before 8PM. Annie was having a total I-don't-feel-good meltdown and wanted no parts of putting on her coat, Clark was having a total I-don't-want-to-leave meltdown and was both hitting me and screaming at me, and I was having a total I-don't-know-how-the-flip-to-handle-parenthood-somedays meltdown and was bawling. Poor Jonathan. Haha! Real life, folks, real life.

---

1. Sound about right, Dad B? Love you, and your always heartfelt tears!
2. Laughter, on the other hand, not at all reserved! Mom has these hilarious *fits* of laughter that strike at the funniest of times and render her pretty well mute and

paralyzed for a solid five minutes. They're the absolute best! Just ask her to tell you the story of the cicada who decided to take a walk with her and Ashley…

3. …or whatever you call getting out of bed at 6AM after not sleeping because your toddler has himself confused for a rooster. The first words out of his mouth one day shortly after Annie arrived were, "Hello, chickens!" No lie, guys!

4. Apparently, overreacting to unlikely and/or unexpected situations involving babies is in my genetics. Once, when her firstborn was only a few months old and was secured in his high chair (thank God), Alicia went out into her garage to grab something from the freezer and inadvertently locked herself out of the house. Two, frantic 911 calls and a broken window later… using a metal garden shovel, I'm told… she and Tristan were reunited safely. In Ashley's world, she and her eldest took a nasty tumble down the (wooden) stairs when he was rather new. Bryce's fall was mild as Ash took all of the blunt force and cradled his landing, but my sister was in total freak-out mode as she sobbed incoherently to a 911 dispatcher. Bryce was fine. You should've seen the bruise on Ashley's butt, though. It was unreal (and something I wish I would have photographed, in retrospect… ha!).

5. Don't fret, everyone, as nothing was *wrong* with Annie at all. My instincts as a nurse were right in every way… it was definitely blood that I saw in Annie's poo. It just wasn't *her* blood. Remember my torn nipple and Annie-the-Cannibal? Yep, the blood I found was *my* blood… after Annie's little body had digested it, that is. Double yum!

6. My best explanation for these silly, unprovoked tears are a concept I have coined the Evil Evening. We will spend an entire chapter on this phenomenon soon enough!

6   THE BLESSING AND CURSE OF VISITORS

To those of you who visited me, cooked for me, cleaned for me, or simply came to snuggle the latest mini-version of me following the births of either Clark or Annie, know that I love you, I appreciate you, and I am glad that you were a part of their beginning. If you read this chapter and leave it feeling hurt or thinking that you should've given Jonathan and I more space when we welcomed our wee ones into the world, you are mishearing what I am about to say. You were, and always will be, valued. If you haven't figured it out yet, though... it's all the baggage and the not-so-good stuff that comes with the good stuff that isn't exactly desirable. In the case of becoming a parent and managing the sudden influx of visitors, this includes stuff like fatigue, embarrassment, jealousy, immodesty, and stress. I wouldn't have sent my own visitors away at any point to free myself of this "stuff", but I would also be a big-old-liar if I didn't acknowledge that it was there. Often.

At the time Clark was born, the hospital we delivered in had a fairly strict policy on visitors. There were set visiting hours, age restrictions, and a limit of no more than four visitors per patient room at any given time. Prior to delivery, allowing four visitors at a time seemed generous. After delivery, however, there were times when we legitimately had to let people back to see us in shifts. It was super-humbling, semi-comical and a tad suffocating all at the same time. At one point, it was so nuts that we had *my* sisters, mom, and aunt, *Jonathan's* aunt, uncle and three cousins, AND three of our best friends (that's twelve people) all there to lay eyes, and hands, on our little bundle-of-love. While Jonathan and I certainly needed some community and a sense of connection with the world beyond our hospital room, the constant presence of others was tiring and, at times, overwhelming.

Sometimes, things can be overwhelming because they are unexpected. Do you want to hear a super weird thing I experienced both in the hospital and at home that really caught me off guard and surprised me? Jealousy. Yup, at times, I felt flat out *jealous* of even the closest of loved ones when they held my baby. As ridiculous as it sounds, all the snuggles they enjoyed cut into those precious moments that *I* felt entitled to. The funniest example of this was the first time Alicia's middle daughter, Sydney, came to the house to meet Clark. At the time, Sydney was the cutest, tiniest, meekest little almost-three-year-old, but when she sat on my couch holding Clark, I felt true, uncomfortable jealousy. My niece was on cloud nine—she'd been carrying around baby dolls on her hip since basically the day she could walk and this one was *real*—and all the while I was counting the seconds until I could have my baby back. Big of me, right?! Obviously I knew that Clark was mine at the end of the day, and I totally laugh at myself now when I look back on these sentiments with hindsight, but jealousy was, in truth, a part of those first day realities.

Another one that caught me by surprise? Embarrassment. Everyone knows that babies cry. Even babies know that babies cry. Watch a barely-walking toddler carry around a doll for a few moments, and you'll know what I mean. Instinctively, he or she will shove bottles and pacifiers into the baby's mouth and rock the doll while saying things like "shhh" or "Waa! Waa!". Despite knowing that my baby was going to cry, I didn't know my baby was going to cry *so much*, and I certainly didn't know that I would end up feeling weirdly ashamed of it.

In those first days and weeks, we had our share of visits during which Clark screamed, or at least fussed, the majority of the time. Sometimes, it was just a timing thing and, unfortunately, he was either overly tired or hungry when folks arrived. Other times, though? Who knows. Babies are super unpredictable and can go from completely chill to inconsolable in seconds. When Clark would cry for our guests, it often left me feeling like a clueless, incapable mother who didn't know what her child needed, especially when those guests would insert little opinions or suggestions for me. Here are some of my "favorites":

- "Do you think he's hungry, honey?"

- "Oh, I bet he's just got a tummy full of gas!"

- "My babies always liked to be held like this..."

You get the picture.

While I know that intentions were always good and that the hearts of my loved ones were in the right place, sometimes as a new parent you simply don't want third party input on caring for your child. Jonathan's pet peeve was when our guests would just assume that we'd appreciate them changing diapers for us. As he'd head for the changing table with Clark and someone would say something akin to, "Oh, let me get that for you!", he'd have to bite his tongue so that he wouldn't respond in a snarky manner. Jonathan didn't want or need someone else to change his child's diaper for him, even if it was for the twentieth time already that day. He was more than capable and preferred, actually, to do it himself. (I struck gold with this guy, I know!)

Before we had children, bringing guests into our home was welcomed because I, the planner, could plan ahead. What a novel concept. Ninety-nine percent of the time, I knew how many folks were coming, when to expect them, for approximately how long they'd be staying, and what activities would fill the evening (be it conversation, a movie, games, food, etc.). As a new mom, however, this couldn't have been further from the case when it came to visitors. Jonathan and I were so insanely tired in the beginning that we barely knew what day of the week it was let alone who was coming when. And a plan? Ha ha. As much as I wished, hoped, and prayed that Clark would sleep in silence while our loved ones ogled over him, this was very, very seldom the case. In being a fan of control and executable plans, bringing guests into my home with a newborn who threw each and every plan out the window was challenging—and just plain embarrassing, if I'm being honest—for Type A me.

Embarrassment came for me in other forms, too, in the newborn days. This was especially notable in the sense of modesty. When it comes to modesty, I grew up in a house with two older sisters who were anything *but* modest. After showering, Alicia and Ashley would stand butt naked in their bedrooms (with the doors wide open practically) while getting ready. Me? I'd take my clothes into the bathroom with me and would turn fifty shades of red if I ever got walked in on. I took this seriously enough that I actually jerry-rigged a lock for the bathroom door (ours didn't work) by opening the drawer closest to it when I wanted seclusion. We had one bathroom for five people, three of which were teenage girls. Both of my sisters lacked any sense of privacy, frequently barged in on my bathroom time, and made statements to younger, powerless me such as "You don't have anything we haven't already seen." Ugh.

While they talked openly about body functions and processes, I, right here, am the girl who would've rather died than ask her mother how to insert a tampon, did it oh-so-wrong the first time by leaving the applicator in place, and hard core passed out right in front of an audience of her female family members. My mom and aunt had sympathy on my horrified little soul. Alicia and Ashley, though? They laughed so, so, SO hard at me (even as I lay on the floor recovering, mind you) and continue to do so any time this "milestone" is remembered. What does all of this signify at the end of the day? I'm a modest person by nature. You know what makes modesty a challenge? Breastfeeding. You know what makes breastfeeding, which is already a *huge* challenge, even more challenging? Visitors.

When you are learning how to breastfeed, modesty is next to impossible. Yes, there are frocks, and vests, and drapes, and canopies, and covers... but when you have no idea what you're doing and are nipple-length-challenged, such as me, you kind of need to be able to *see* what the heck is happening in the frontal region. Add in all of the extras that we talked about previously—things like shields, pillows, creams, collectors, and pumps—and breastfeeding in the presence of visitors is awkward at best.

I can remember so many guests telling me things like "Go ahead and nurse the baby!" or "We don't mind if you need to feed him!" Well guess what, folks, *I* minded. If feeding a newborn was a quick, simple thing, being a modest mommy would be no big deal. You don't want your father-in-law sitting across the room while the girls are on full display? No worries! Just ask him to step out for a few minutes until the baby has eaten and then there will be *loads* of time for visiting. Ummm... no. How often do babies eat? Oh, right. Every two to three hours. How long do those initial feedings sometimes last? Oh, ya. FOREVER. Working around a boob schedule when it comes to newborns and visitors is just no fun. Plain and simple.

Speaking of schedules, another schedule that comes into play in terms of babies and guests is that of the sleep/wake schedule. We've already discussed the concept that although babies might not sleep for *long*, per se, they do tend to sleep *often*. If you're a control freak, like me, you will yearn for the smallest taste of a schedule in the worst way after bringing your baby home. Because of this, establishing a routine, even if super-duper rudimentary, will be something you strive for basically as soon as your brain can process thoughts more advanced than like "feed baby", "feed self", or "change diaper" (you may laugh, mommies-to-be, but it's going to happen...*). When Jonathan and I would finally succeed in feeding Clark and getting him to sleep, we wanted him to... duh... sleep! Just like in the hospital, it never failed that right about the moment Clark dozed off soundly outside of our arms (for a change), a car would pull into the driveway.

Visitors don't like to look at sleeping babies. Visitors like to *hold* sleeping babies. This, in turn, resulted in me being all-sorts of stressed. I'd either ask our guests to wait until Clark woke, which left us in this crazy-awkward state of limbo, or give them the go-ahead (*if* they even asked first) to pick Clark up while holding my breath and praying to Jesus that He would be gracious enough to keep the sleep. Most of the time, thankfully, Clark continued to snooze away and I remained untethered for a few moments more... just long enough to shovel some of whatever food-related-goodness our guests often brought into my mouth.

Before I go any further about food-entailed visits, let me just say that edibles of *any* sort are always welcomed by new moms and dads. When you are exhausted beyond your wildest dreams and living in the state of delirium that comes with bringing home a newborn, remembering that you even *need* to eat is an accomplishment, let alone actually planning for and preparing meals. This being said, however, food visits do require some communication in the realm of details. Things like....What time is drop off? Will said food arrive hot or require heating/cooking? Is "drop off" *really* drop off, or are you staying for a visit and/or to dine with us? Important things to know. At times, even those visitors toting the giant-est of casseroles and most sinful of cakes caused me stress merely because details weren't clearly communicated, or there were incorrect assumptions. Before having a baby, it may not be overly essential to know the intentions behind someone telling you that they are "dropping by with dinner". After baby, though, when life is consumed by the long and endless feeding cycles we've already talked about at length, you kind of need to know (or at least *deserve* to know) whether "dropping by" means hanging for two minutes or two hours… especially when you're tired, hormonal, and hungry.

I think it's pretty safe to say that my crankiest moments in life are those when I am either tired, hungry, or a combination of both. Jonathan, my mom, and my sisters would attest to this as truth[1]. For basically the entire beginning of your newborn's life, you're going to be in some form of both of these states like 24/7. The fatigue part was pretty obvious and undeniable to me, Jonathan, and anyone within a 40-foot radius of myself for a good month (or six) after my babies arrived. I looked about as tired as I felt. The hunger part, however, was different than I expected it to be.

Before I had Clark, I'll be completely honest and say that I was oddly excited to spend a few days in the hospital where others would wait on me hand and foot and food—that I selected from a menu—would be delivered to my bedside. This didn't sound like such a bad gig. In reality, guys, I think I maybe ate a grand total of three bites of whatever I even ordered during my entire stay. For starters, I was so, so tired. Like too tired to even look at food, let alone eat it. It was a weird experience, but when food was placed before me, I almost had to give my brain a few minutes to recognize its existence and recall the basic process of eating. Bizarre. Then, there was the whole shift in priorities when I became a parent. When you have someone else's needs to see to first, believe me when I say that your own take a backseat… a super, way back there, backseat. In the beginning, until Jonathan and I settled into a little bit of a routine and semi-figured-out what we were doing, I think we got to a point of being so overwhelmed with everything else, visitors included, that we forgot to acknowledge our own hunger. Unfortunately for us, however, just because our brains didn't acknowledge our hunger didn't mean that the crank-nasties which often accompany our hunger were lost. They were there, making all of the other stuff just…worse.

I've been spending some time reflecting on my own experiences with visitors in the newborn days, and there is one specific memory that keeps coming to me. It's a story that sort of illustrates and encompasses practically all of the guest-struggles I've mentioned so far. One day, very early on in the days of Clark, Jonathan and I received either a phone call or a text (I can't recall which) from his super-dear Aunt Peg saying that she, her husband,

Skip, and her daughter, Lisa, wanted to bring us a meal and sneak a peek at Clark. Of course, we were more than happy for them to do so, and it just so happened that this worked out perfectly as Jonathan's Grandma, Nadean, didn't drive and had been bursting at the seams to spend some time with her "dear and precious great-grandson", as she referred to him[2]. In order for Grandma to spend a day with Clark and me, I planned to pick her up after her next Reach Out meeting (Grandma was more social and lively, even in her last weeks as an 87-year-old, than I have ever been, mind you), and since she lived only a few houses away from Uncle Skip and Aunt Peg, they had agreed to take her home after their drop-in. Score!

The day of Grandma's visit arrived, I picked her up, and we managed to get back to the house without too much of a fuss from Clark. Jonathan was away at work, Grandma was in her glory as she snuggled Clark on the couch—between feedings of course—and I took advantage of her presence by pumping, vacuuming, and attempting to accomplish other small things around the house... things that I normally wasn't capable of completing (easily anyway) without a second set of hands. We spent several hours together, but the time went quickly and was a joy. You know how it is, though, guys. After lots of time together with someone, even if it's your best friend in the entire world, there comes a point when you're ready for whatever is "normal". This was especially true for me after Jonathan returned home and we were ready to just settle down for the evening. A short time after the hubby got home from work, Skip, Peg, and Lisa arrived for what I assumed was going to be a semi-brief visit so that they could get Grandma home and enjoy their own dinners. What *they* had anticipated, however, was something different...something more like holding Clark while Jonathan and I ate *our* dinner. Right then. With an audience.

Although it wasn't what I had in mind or had expected, this change in plans may have been OK if it weren't for two things. Number one: the Evil Evening, which I will elaborate upon in the next chapter. Stay tuned. Number two: a hungry baby. Clark was pretty fussy from the time our guests arrived, and because I knew he was wanting to be fed, it wasn't something that was going to just be willed, shushed, or snuggled away. Remember modest me? Well, I wasn't about to bust out my boobs in front of an onslaught of onlookers. Instead, I scooped up my little one and prepared to head upstairs where I would feed him in isolation.

Because I knew that feeding Clark would take quite a while, I thought that my comments explaining this truth might encourage our relatives to wrap up their visit and head home. Instead—and honestly, with the *best* of intentions—Jonathan and I were told that they would wait. While this was meant to be thoughtful and helpful so that my poor husband and I could enjoy a warm dinner for once while someone else worried about Clark's comfort, it, instead, put a tremendous amount of pressure on me. I felt as though I had to rush through a feeding, a subsequent pumping, and then force-feed myself in front of watchful eyes. Not appealing.

I'd like to tell you that I handled this situation with poise, maturity, and grace... but that would be the furthest of exaggerations. Know what I actually did? I sat in my bed, attempted to feed Clark while crying like a child, and begged my husband to somehow make our family members disappear. At the end of the day, we all survived and it was all really no big deal, but the amount of stress that I took away from this visit was so much more than what it should have been. (This text should be inserted along with the other footnotes below, but I'm keeping it right here—front and center—so that it isn't missed by a certain few sets of eyes who I am sure will read this book because they love and support me. Aunt Peg, Uncle Skip, and Lisa: I know you guys have got to be feeling horrified right about now. I was beyond hormonal, tired, and at a point of irrationality when you visited. I love you each so, so much. Please laugh at my utter silliness. Don't be hard on yourselves at all! You are the absolute *best*.)

If you are currently pregnant, my hope is that perhaps in reading about *my* realities in Visitor Land, you will be willing to have honest conversations and convey clear expectations with your loved ones so that *your* visits go a tad smoother... and if nothing else, at least you'll anticipate the not-so-smooth. In encountering and reflecting upon all of these uncomfortable, stress-inducing experiences with guests in the days after Clark was born, I was so much readier for them the second time around.

When it came to Annie, however, there wasn't the mass amount of attention. Firstborns get it all, you'll learn. From their own parents, firstborns get pregnancies done "right", always-clean clothing (even if it means five wardrobe changes a day because of poop or spit up crises), and pacifiers that are sanitized each and every time they pop out of baby's mouth. From loved ones, firstborns get hospital visits, and home visits, and *second* home visits...

and all the while Mom and Dad score lots of lasagnas and chocolate cakes. Subsequent babies? Well, it's all minimized from there. I only made it to two and already found myself cutting (all) corners when I was pregnant the second time around, making statements like "Eh. It's just a tiny spot of poop.", and following the Five Second Rule for loose pacifiers far more often than I'd like to admit. While we had literal lines of guests in the hospital after delivering Clark, visitors were much scarcer when it came to Annie, even after we made it home. We still received lots of love, don't get me wrong, but it was less in quantity and in every way different.

For starters, I was jealous of no one. I knew I'd be the one seeing my girl at 3AM for at least nine weeks (which turned out to be nine months), and that was good enough for me. Then, there was the whole "holding a sleeping baby" thing. Whatever, folks! My hands were already more-than-full with a certain male toddler that if someone offered to hold Annie for a few minutes, even if she had just fallen asleep in her Pack 'N Play, or crib, or *wherever*, I would've been like "God bless you!".

Remember how I was embarrassed if Clark cried during visits? HAHAHA! Although I *will* say that Annie basically didn't cry, ever, for the first two to three weeks of her life (totally the opposite of her brother), I could've cared less how she behaved. Appearances no longer mattered to me. Plain and simple, I was just trying to survive being outnumbered by my offspring (how you saints/nutters with, like, four, five, or ten kids live to tell the tale is beyond me). And then, arguably the biggest change in me from Baby One to Baby Two? Modesty, shmodesty. If you're coming to *my* house to see *my* baby, you may very well see *my* boobs. Not comfortable with that? Guess what, guys, there are other rooms for you to sit in until I'm done, which may not be for a good 45 minutes. Ha. Oh, how things change.

I'm not one for providing explicitly defined "tips" as I am, by no means, a pro at (even surviving) parenting. I do, however, have some loosely-termed-suggestions for both new parents and baby-snugglers alike. They are as follows…

Moms and Dads:

- There are going to be times when your baby screams for no good reason at all, and this has nothing to do with what you do or don't know how to do. Babies cry. Lots. Visitors *expect* babies to cry. Lots. Give yourselves grace, and let go of hoping for quiet, peaceful visits. The truth? They will be few and far between... basically for the rest of your lives.

- If you're a control freak like me, accepting help doesn't always come easily or naturally. Just like growing a baby bump elicits all sorts of unsought advice and offers of assistance, actually *having* the baby does too. Maybe you want to figure out the newborn stuff for yourself and don't necessarily want someone else scooping up your wee one or telling you what *he* or *she* thinks baby needs. That's OK! If your idea of a helping hand is merely someone folding that load of laundry that's been sitting in the dryer for hours (days?) or running the vacuum cleaner every now and again... speak up. You'd be surprised at how willing your loved ones are to help you in whatever way best serves *you* in the moment.

- Have a soundly sleeping baby and a growing queue of eager-to-cuddle guests? *You* are the parent, and *you* know what is best for your child. It is true that in the early weeks, most babies can sleep through practically anything, including a change in position from laying to being picked up and held. (It may have taken a song and dance to *get* Clark to sleep, but once he was there, I'm pretty sure a nuclear bomb wouldn't have phased him.) This being said, however, it's also perfectly acceptable for you to keep your guests waiting or even ask for a rain check if that's what is best for you and your little one.

- Is your babe ready to eat in a house packed with visitors? You do you! If you're cool with the idea of breastfeeding in front of an audience, go for it! Anyone who is lacking in comfort can (and will—believe me) quickly dismiss themselves from observing. If you prefer or just simply require isolation, however, be bold and tell your loved ones that they need to scoot... at least until your bundle is a few notches more content and all body parts have served their purpose and are again hidden from the light of day.

- The bottom line is that *you* call the shots on visitors. If you don't want folks coming to the hospital at all or even prefer a few days of alone-time at home before anyone lays eyes and hands on your baby... it's really OK. Communicate these things clearly, and early, and with your head held high. Of course, you *can* get through the newborn stage independently, but let me just tell you that the help of others— in whatever way or ways work best for *you*—can be a saving grace for new parents. Be honest with your loved ones, and when they want to visit, try to find a way to make it beneficial for everyone.

Visitors:

- Make no assumptions, and communicate clearly! Clarify your intentions for a visit from the start. Believe me when I say that the difference between a 10 minute visit versus an hour-long visit in the world of a new, exhausted, hormonal, yearning-for-routine mom or dad is *huge*.

- Provide options. Don't be afraid to say things like: "We can either bring your dinner hot and hold the baby while you eat, or we can bring it cold so you can pop it in the oven at a time that is most convenient for you."

- If baby is sleeping comfortably outside of Mom's or Dad's arms when you arrive, it's totally appreciated when you make statements similar to "I don't want to wake him/her!" Chances are, you'll be told to go ahead and pick up the baby anyway, but if you're not... you've just lightened the load on a new parent's shoulders significantly.

- While quick visits and the concept of "dropping and running" may be rude at some points in life, the newborn period is simply not one of them. Be flexible, read your loved ones' verbal and non-verbal cues, and don't feel you're being rude if it makes more sense for you to leave and visit again in a few days, or weeks, when everyone is a little better rested and adjusted. There's nothing wrong with lots of on-the-shorter-side visits…especially when edibles are in tow. (Oh, and unless your loved one is some sort of weirdo or has an allergy, it's really, really hard to go wrong with chocolate.)

When you're a new parent who is heavily deprived in the sleep department, adjusting to an entirely new way of living, and just trying to keep your head above water from minute to minute, it's not difficult to see why visits can be stressful and overwhelming. Despite this, drop-ins really can be welcomed, pleasant, and, best of all, helpful. The biggest take-away from everything I've shared and said about visitors is this: Anticipate, communicate, and enjoy! Soon enough these early, guest-filled days will be a thing of the past and you'll be left to survive the struggles alone… and without a stash of frozen casseroles to lean on when meal planning is a mountain you just don't feel like climbing.

---

1. Seeing as how my three-year-old is becoming more and more perceptive, I would also now add him to this list. Just like being a newborn mom is hard, being a toddler mom is too. Trying not to yell at my children 24 hours a day is a very real, current day struggle for me, and if I'm tired or hungry? Forget about it. Just the other day after a little bit of a Mommy Meltdown, Clark looked at me and said, "Do you need to rest, Mommy?" You betcha, bud.

2. Sadly, Grandma passed away only a handful of weeks after her namesake, Annie Nadean, was born to Jonathan and I. Grandma was special beyond words to the both of us and talked up her loved ones to a completely comical level. In fact, Jonathan and I used to play a game when we received cards or thank you notes from Grandma, which was basically every week. The game involved betting on how many adjectives would be contained inside her always handwritten messages, and the closest to the actual number was the winner. I think Grandma's record was 37. Obviously, she *loved* her family, which is something that hasn't been lost on her offspring. Only a few days ago, Jonathan and I had his dad and stepmom over for dinner. Here is the actual thank you text we received afterwards: "Thank you so very much for an absolutely fantastic evening last night!!! The dinner was totally amazing… shrimp was so very naturally flavorful, french onion soup was the best I've ever had, and the main course of chicken Chesapeake was out of this world!!! And, of course we totally loved the incredibly delicious raspberry brownies and ice cream!! You guys are the best!!! Thank you so much!!!! Love you all so much!!!" Like Mother, like Son.

7   EVIL EVENINGS

Things can be scary when they are new and different. Things can be boatloads scari*er* when they are new and different AND unpredictable. To the dismay of every Type A Personality out there, like myself, newborns are about as far from predictable as a thing can get. Be it 2AM or 2PM those first, long, delirious days, and you've got yourself a crapshoot of "what ifs" and what sometimes truly feels like survival of the fittest. Babies are demanding without warning, without schedule, and without provocation… both day and night and everywhere in between. Even with a cup of highly-caffeinated coffee on board and in circulation, a few hours of "sleep" on the internal register, and the good vibes of the sun's rays beaming through opened curtains and windowpanes, daytime hours with a newborn, on their own, can be draining and overwhelming. The *overnight* hours, though? Oh man, they're just extra rough. Babies' overnight needs have a way of feeling super overwhelming, super, super fast.

Is it just me, or have you ever noticed that nighttime, in general, makes everything worse? Pretend, for example, that you've got a job interview tomorrow. Now to bedazzle things a bit, let's say you're a techie nerd, like my hubby, and this is the Job of Jobs. Your dream job. Think along the lines of Apple or Google… something "big time" that you've spent lots of time researching and preparing for. You go over some possible interview scenarios in your head throughout the day, you use your commute for talking yourself through a run-through, and you even have the hubby serve as a makeshift interviewer to grill you with questions over dinner. You're antsy and nervous, but it's in a good way and is nothing you can't handle—until evening approaches, that is. As the sun says "adios!" and bids another day farewell, your *good* nerves go *bad*. Butterflies in the belly turn to unease, which turns to true anxiety, doubt, and fear. Suddenly, you question whether or not you should even show up for the interview. You wonder whether or not you have what it takes. You fear that you're going to make yourself look like an idiot in a room full of Steve Jobs-es. And your mind races, and races, and races.

For whatever reason, life's stresses have a way of being exaggerated and emblazoned in our minds under the cover of darkness. Just recently, this phenomenon was in full effect for me as I laid awake one evening worrying about my kids. As a mom, this happens kind of a lot. It's just a part of who I am. Going out for a few hours is one thing, but being away from Clark and Annie overnight is a whole different concept. It *requires* a lot of planning (my specialty, as you know) and doesn't-exactly-require yet always *includes* fretting.

Jonathan and I do make a point of taking a good bit of couple time and even alone time for ourselves as we fully recognize that it makes us better parents, spouses, and people in general. Being away from the kids overnight, though? As I write this, Annie is just shy of 20 months old and Clark is approaching three and a half. I can count on one hand (maybe two for Clark) the amount of times I've slept away from them. A few weeks ago, however, Jonathan and I were slated to go away for an entire weekend with our friends Bryan and Kelly. Our plans were to travel about two hours north and stay in my father-in-law's creekside cottage. Formally christened "Lazy Acres" and informally just "the cottage", this cozy, little abode has sort of become a home away from home for Jonathan and I since we got married almost nine years ago[1]. We figured that if we were going to be brave and get away for <u>more</u> <u>than</u> <u>one</u> night (gasp!), "the cottage" was the place to give it a go.

In the *days* leading up to our getaway, I was busy taking care of the kids, writing up instructions and suggested schedules (told you, guys... Type A), prepping meals, and everything else that overbearing mothers do. I was stressed, don't get me wrong, but I simply didn't have a ton of time to sit around and stress. The *nights*, though? Gah! As soon as my head hit the pillow, my brain was bombarded with anxious thoughts like:

- "What if one of the kids gets sick[2] or hurt?"

- "What if it snows and Jonathan and I get stuck away from home?"

- "What if Clark can't fall asleep because his OCD bedtime routine is disrupted?"

- "What if the kids are just awful, jerky toddlers the entire time we're gone?"

- "What if *I* can't handle being more than a quick drive away from my kids and have a Mommy freak-out?"

The worries kept piling one on top of the other into a heap of ugly (in noun form) that seemed daunting until morning dawned. After I got some rest and daylight shone on the situation, I felt more at ease. When evening returned again as our getaway approached, however? So did the yuck.

In the realm between dusk and nighttime, it seems, my mind has a way of blowing small things out of proportion. Thankfully, this only happens on occasion and is something I typically deal with just at times of high stress. After my kiddos were born, though? This *sometimes*-occurring surge of worry became an *always*-occurring tidal wave of uncertainty to the Nth degree. I lovingly (sarcasm) refer to this concept as the "Evil Evening". As best I can describe it, the Evil Evening is like a Pandora's box of nonsense— anxiety, fatigue, stress, worry, and anticipation—that "magically" opens when the sun sets on a hormonally-wrecked new mom. It looks and feels a lot like a switch that can take you from a state of feeling accomplished, a tad-bit-put-together and:

- "OK! I got this!"

to experiencing a sense of impending doom for what another long, sleepless night may hold and:

- "Crap! I totally *don't* got this!"

After I had Clark, I remember telling my mom that evenings, for some reason, felt scary. I could experience as good of a day as was possible with a newborn, start to feel like I was finally getting the swing of being a mom to the point of actually enjoying it, and then 5PM would roll around and all of these gross emotions would start setting in. Harry Potter groupie, like me? If so—picture the Dementors and the way they were depicted in the film series[3]. Things could be totally OK in The Land of Mom, evening would hit, and out of nowhere a Dementor would eerily creep up on me only to steal my joy and leave fear in its wake. My Evil Evenings may not have been quite as dramatic as the masterful, dark creatures of J.K. Rowling, but they for sure felt *real* and could completely upend any remote feelings of control that I was starting to grasp as a new mom.

Sometimes, these weird, Evil Evenings would put me in unexplainable, almost ridiculous, tears. The time I sat down with Jonathan for dinner only to burst into hysterics for no good reason at all? The Evil Evening at work. Other times, the Evil Evening would give me knots in my stomach. I can remember a few occasions, for example, when I had been badly looking forward to Jonathan's return from work and a chance to reconnect over a good meal[4] only to find that the approach of dusk and the arrival of the Evil Evening had robbed me of an appetite. At a couple of points in time, the Evil Evening even brought me to random outbursts of gut-wrenching laughter… which may have resulted in my less-hormonal husband questioning the status of my sanity. You know what, though? I might have looked pretty crazy laughing at nothing or next-to-nothing, but I celebrated the evenings that ended in laughter instead of tears for a change. The Evil Evening had landed me in a weird place as a new parent. In this place, my emotions were totally and completely labile, *especially* in the post-afternoon hours.

When I shared with my mom that I was experiencing this silly, almost-phobia of dusk and the nighttime that followed it, she was quick to tell me that I wasn't alone. Even though nearly 28 years had passed since bringing her youngest daughter into the world (that would be me…), she could vividly remember having the same feelings. In the early days of motherhood, my mom shared that as the sun went down, her level of anxiety went up. Mom dreaded those long, lonely newborn nights, and she very much welcomed the rising of the sun every morning. The Evil Evening was a real thing for her, too.

Before I sat down to start writing this chapter, I knew that at least my mom and I had a rocky relationship with the evening hours as new parents. As I thought a little harder on the subject, however, I remembered a funny story that suggested to me it may be a more universal experience. When Jonathan and I participated in childbirth classes before the arrival of Clark, the instructor shared with us a candid memory of her own newborn days. While, like me, she never dealt with postpartum depression and was quick to point new moms towards medical help if they ever felt hopeless or lacked a sense of connection with their baby, she did recall crying lots in the days— and especially evenings— following the births of her children. Our instructor shared that once, as dusk fell, she happened to be looking at her curtains. Yes, her curtains. Without warning or explanation, tears began to fall from her cheeks. When her husband looked at her, bewildered and concerned, to ask what was the matter… she turned to him and laugh-cried while explaining that their curtains just weren't the "right color". Ha! Stinking Evil Evening.

As I prepared for this project and attempted to gauge the newborn experience for moms and dads across the board, I came upon many a discussion page and article where things like "weepy evenings" and "nighttime anxiety" were brought up. The case of the Evil Evening, it seems, goes well beyond just myself, my mom, and my childbirth instructor. In all actuality, lots and lots of new parents encounter some version of it. I have a couple of (very loosely defined) theories on why, perhaps, this phenomenon occurs *as* and *when* it does.

For starters, there are simply less distractions when it comes to the evening and nighttime hours. During the day, especially when you are the sole provider for your wee one if your support person has returned to work, there are just lots of things to (try to) accomplish. You've got to feed your cherub, snag some snuggle time, feed yourself, shower (if only…), and attempt to check off maybe one or two of the items on your list of like 45 that could be beneficial in keeping your household standing for another day. There's just so much to do when the sun is shining.

As the sun fades west, however, and the day winds down? Well, there's less to keep a mind occupied. When the body is busy, the brain is distracted and focused on the task at hand. When the body slows down or attempts to rest, though? The brain is free to worry, and stress, and anticipate. This is true for everyone, I think, but it is *especially* true for new parents because of the added stressors of sleep deprivation and adaptation to life with a newborn. For postpartum moms, in particular, it's *especially*-especially true because of the added "wonder" of hormones. These special, blessed hormones have a way of making a new mom look and feel like a loon at any time of day really, but the evenings? Well, hormones are just mean, spiteful little buggers that exaggerate baseline anxieties and prevent any semblance of rest when the day comes to a close.

Then, when you've been home alone all day with a little one who doesn't really interact and can't hold a conversation with you (no offense, babies of the world), there is a sense of relief and release when your "other" returns to you… which most often occurs in the evening. If I'm being honest, Jonathan getting home from work those first weeks after Clark joined our family was a little weird. I anticipated his arrival so much and for so long during the day, and then he would show up and I'd suddenly feel like a basket-case who was constantly on the verge of tears.

For me, my husband is just "my person" if you know what I mean. If I'm going to let myself be vulnerable and truly seen to anyone, it's Jonathan. He's my rock, and he supports me and my dreams (and even my failures) without ceasing. Because being a new mom was so hard and so different and so Weltschmerz-y[5]—especially during the solo daytime hours—I sort of had a tendency to dump a day's worth of thoughts, frustrations, and happenings on my man not long after he walked back through the door. It was like my emotions were carbonated and capped tightly in a glass bottle all day long while it was just me and my unable-to-chat babe. As soon as my hubby came back to me, however, and I had someone to converse and commiserate with… that cap was cracked, my feelings were free, and out they erupted. Whether I wanted them to or not.

Finally, what may be the most obvious explanation for the Evil Evening is the reality that it affects baby, too. All of the parents out there already know this to be true, but babies are often fussiest in the evening hours. Be it true colic[6] or general crankiness, lots of newborns cry most during the evening… right around the time you and your man are longing to re-connect and enjoy a nice, quiet (hahaha!!) dinner after being apart for the day[7]. Some folks even refer to this time of the day as the "witching hours". Well, when your newborn is crying, and crying, and crying despite your best attempts at isolating reasons why (Are you wet? Are you tired? Are you hungry? Are you bored?)… it isn't that surprising that a new mom may also start to feel anxious, overwhelmed, and a bit gloomy herself.

Jonathan may not have delivered Clark and may not have had a body ravaged by postnatal hormones, but even he, I would say, was hit by the Evil Evening on occasion. I can remember one specific evening a few weeks into parenting when we had a very fussy, almost hostile little Clark on our hands (Clark came about as close to having colic as one can get without an official diagnosis… Annie was much easier. Thank you, Lord!). I was vacuuming not because my floors needed to be cleaned, but because my brain couldn't process the sound of crying any longer without a breakdown. Jonathan was bouncing Clark on his shoulder for what seemed like hours (it was probably more like 30 minutes), and I'll never forget him looking at his tiny little son with tears in his own eyes. Frustration and helplessness were painted all over his face when he said to Clark, "What do you *need*, buddy? Why can't I help you?" It broke my heart and obviously, his as well.

Whatever may be the source of this strange happening, it is super real to many new parents. All of the medical folks out there, my fellow nurses in particular, will appreciate that I liken this phenomenon to "sundowning". If you aren't familiar with the concept of sundowning, it is a stark change in a person's behavior that usually occurs as the day is transitioning to night. Sundowning most often affects those with Alzheimer's disease and other forms of dementia, but I even saw it as a floor nurse in patients with no prior history because of the stress associated with a hospital stay. Picture Joe Schmoe, whose daytime-self is the sweetest, gentlest, meekest elderly gentleman you've ever laid eyes on, having an almost Hulk-like experience as the sun sets. The new Joe? Angry, violent, and stronger than even looks possible for his delicate frame. Every nurse has a good sundowning story in their back pocket. For me, I don't even need to look beyond the mirror because my Evil Evenings gave me plenty of personal examples.

I remember the Evil Evening hitting me like a ton of bricks on one particular occasion when I bit off a little more than I could chew too soon after Annie's delivery. Annie was born just nine days before my family's annual Memorial Day bash. Every year, this event is hosted by my brother-in-law's wonderful Dad and Stepmom, Jon and Kendra, who are like another set of grandparents to our kids. It's always a time of games and crafts for the tots, much-needed conversation and laughter amongst the adults, and good food and drink for all. We may have been beyond-tired and still adjusting to life as a family of four, but Jonathan and I made the decision to go. For *our* sakes, Jonathan and I really needed to get out of the house and escape the monotony of the newborn routine. For *Clark's* sake, he was needing a little attention and time with his cousins as his entire world had been turned upside down. All in all, we had a great time, and even though my mom and sisters thought I was a little nuts and were pretty surprised by my appearance, we made the right choice in going.

Clark was busy, busy, busy and kept us on our toes, but he behaved about as well as he could for being an always-moving toddler (nothing has changed, by the way, ask anyone who knows him). Besides her typical latching struggles, Annie didn't make much of a fuss and slept basically the entire time. Sounds like a win, right? Well, even though everything was going as smoothly as can be expected with two unpredictable, tiny little humans, in a matter of seconds I went from being collected… to an internal wreck. The Evil Evening was upon me *heavy*.

I glanced at Jonathan, caught his attention, and my panicked eyes must have said it all because he knew we needed to start packing up *immediately*. I muttered something along the lines of "We gotta go!", and in a matter of mere moments, we had collected all of our baby gear and gadgets, properly fastened our mini-selves into their car seats, grabbed our to-go plates of cake (you're totally the best, Kendra!), and began the hour-long trek home. A few minutes into the trip, Jonathan gave me a "You OK?", and the waterworks started. I probably cried for a solid half of that trip home for no identifiable reason only to laugh the other half of the trip at my nonsense. All I can say is that I've got some pretty darned-good loved ones who support me, crazy and all, because none of this phased them in the least. They were all just happy that my crew made an appearance in any form, albeit short, and were much obliged to let us escape whenever necessary.

Because having no routine, no schedule, and no predictability took me so far beyond the comforts of my element and my norm those first days with newborns, I knew that I needed not only the support of my family, friends, and Jonathan (especially), but some divine intervention, as well. If spirituality or faith isn't a part of your life or your community, please know that you are both respected and welcomed here! You can still see me, and feel me… differences and all. I hope you'll come along as I share, but if you can't or won't, just skip ahead a paragraph or two. I'll meet you for the wrap-up!

As I briefly mentioned before, prayer is a basic source of strength for me in my day to day life. It's sort of a calming, centering, focusing thing that has become central to my adult self. Before kids, I used to keep the radio off in the car and use the solace and quiet as a chance to check-in Above. Since a "quiet car ride" is non-existent in a world after kids, now, I usually pray at length when I am running. Additionally, I often pray in short, out-loud bursts when I'm having "a moment" and need God to help keep me from being imprisoned (or at least very harshly judged)[8].

Prayer was such a crutch for me after the births of both of my babies. When I would sense the Evil Evening in the distance and knew that it was approaching, yet again, I often prayed. I prayed for comfort, I prayed for peace, and I prayed that it would quickly pass. Most of the time, these prayers were internal and brief, but there were times when I actually asked Jonathan if he minded praying with me or was at least OK with me praying out loud right next to him. Many times as a new mom, the Evil Evening just *nagged* at me, bringing with it all kinds of anxiety. Ultimately, however, being in prayer and acknowledging to myself and others that I was having this experience is how I was able to put it in its place and laugh it away instead of becoming overwhelmed or suffocated by it.

For lots and lots of reasons, nighttime with a newborn is just scary. When you've got a baby who won't settle and a body that is t i r e d, every night, in the beginning anyway, feels long, and dark, and unsettling... especially when life before babe was filled with actual (and now coveted after) rest and rejuvenation. When you just can't predict what the night ahead may bring, it's no surprise that the hours leading up to it can feel a little "evil". Fortunately though, the nights *do* get easier, hormones *do* abate, routines *do* emerge, and eternal exhaustion *does* become "normal".

For me, the Evil Evening relented its daily pursuit of my "control" when I was finally able to settle into all of the new normals that life with a newborn threw at me, both times around. Inch by inch, as the unpredictable dusk and nighttime hours became something that I was more accustomed to, ready for, and even challenged-in-a-good-way by sometimes (bring it!!), I was able to greet the evening with more confidence and assurance in myself and with less fear and fret for what may (or may not... such as sleep) come.

When you take an established home with established routines and established schedules and toss into the mix a newborn who is anything but established in any way, it's understandable that life, for a period anyway, is topsy-turvy. Topsy-turvy living, guys, especially as the dark, baby-fuss-filled hours of evening approach, can bring on all sorts of uncharacteristic, Evil Evening outbursts. In time, however, glimpses of predictability and schedule will spring forth like tiny tendrils of green erupting from the soil after a long Winter. When they do and when the Evil Evening fades away? I promise you'll have lots of memories and stories worth laughing about for years and years to come.

---

1. My father-in-law purchased "the cottage" from his best friend, Tom, shortly before Jonathan and I were married. Having acquired an heirloom property just a few doors down from Lazy Acres, Tom and his family focused their attention there and, understandably, let Lazy Acres go uninhabited and without much attention or concern for quite some time. Primarily, my father-in-law made this investment with the intention of creating a legacy property for his sons and (at the time) future grandchildren. He saw a beautiful piece of creek-front land and had dreams of a future, newly constructed dwelling. He also saw a glorified lean-to with a leaking ceiling, a mud-covered floor, and several four-legged inhabitants—a shack, essentially, without a heat source or functional plumbing—and thought, "Yeah, I can save this place until we are at a point to build something new!" Here's what I thought, and even told Jonathan, upon first sight: "I will never, *ever* sleep in that place." Well, my father-in-law is a miracle worker, a true handyman, and a visionary. "The cottage" isn't luxurious, by any means, but it's *home*… for now… and that beats a hot shower any day. Oh, and yes, I've totally slept there. Dozens of times. In fact, I kind of *love* the place.

2. Funny aside: Annie *did* get sick… with the belly bug. The two hours it took to get home were the longest two hours of my life! Another funny aside: The hubby and I actually just solidified plans last night for me to go along with him to a work conference, in *Vegas*, in just a few weeks. I live in PA, guys, so we are talking most of the way across the country. Can you please start praying for me now? Ha! Thank God for my family. Alicia said to me, and I quote, "I promise to take care of your kids even if they are barfing and pooping their guts out." That's love, right there!

3. *Harry Potter and the Prisoner of Azkaban.* Directed by Alfonso Cuarón, Warner Bros. Pictures, 2004.

4. Let it be noted that a *good* meal and a *hot* meal are not synonymous when you are a parent

5. To jog your memory, Weltschmerz is a state of depression that can occur when dreams and realities clash

6. An all-sorts-of-common and no-sorts-of-fun "condition" in which otherwise healthy babies just cry, cry, cry—like *hours* each day—cry. My nephew, Landon, suffered from colic, and, oh my goodness, it was awful. I can remember a time or

two when our whole crew was together for one of my mom's Sunday dinners during which Landon screamed the entire time. Ashley and Kyle were champs, thank God, who quickly learned how to function with a whole lot of background noise and their sanity, somehow, intact. My mom, though? Not so much. Landon's cries, and the inability to console those cries, made her ultra-flustered. It was actually funny to watch how physically uncomfortable she was, and it's still something we make mention of from time to time.

7.   ... *or* when you have family slated to come for a visit. Naturally. If you need a refresher course on how evenings with visitors went for me, anyway, flip back to the last chapter. Not pretty.

8.   Such a "moment" might resemble my toddler looking right at me and acting in defiance for the one thousandth time of the day at 8AM—deep cleansing breath—OK, I'm good.

8   PINT-SIZED TAKEOVER

For being so very tiny, it's both amazing and humorous how newborns completely change every aspect of living. They change the way our homes physically look and logistically function. They change the way we travel, and recreate, and socialize. They change the way we think, make decisions, and prioritize. They even change the way we work and simply "do life" on a day to day basis. It's been a few chapters since I've prepped you with any warnings, so I think we're a tad overdue. Here's one for you: This chapter is kind of a flight-of-thoughts and a little all over the map, if I'm being honest. If you read it and at any point think to yourself, "How on Earth did we get here? Weren't we just talking about _____?"... just know that you didn't miss something or zone out for a couple of paragraphs. The "magical" glue that holds all of what follows together? Babies disrupt orderly lives... from top to bottom. When it comes to newborns, believe me when I say that nothing is sacred or safe or spared from their influence. It's all fair game.

The At-Home Takeover

Let's begin with the overall appearance of one's home. Before we had children, Jonathan and I had some friends over for a visit shortly after we moved into our current address. They had never seen our place before, so we gave them a room by room tour. I had to chuckle when one of our guests, a teenager at the time, asked Jonathan and I, "Where is all your *stuff*?" She simply couldn't wrap her brain around the idea that we didn't have accumulated junk lying around, and it made all of us—her parents especially—laugh. Believe me when I say that having kids means having *stuff*, too. Come on back, Erica. Our place looks a little different these days...

While, yes, there is only so much that a baby actually *needs*... namely, food, diapers, and clothing... there are so many things that are nice to have in helping keep our wee ones safe, comfortable, cute, and entertained. For sleeping and napping, we're talking a crib, a bassinet, a playard, a rocker, swaddles, and sleep sacks. For transport, it's the car seat, car seat base, and baby carrier. In the world of entertainment, you'll need a stroller, a swing, a bouncer, and an abundance of books and toys. For health and safety needs, we're talking monitors, an aspirator, a humidifier, a thermometer, soaps, balms and medications. When it comes to feeding supplies, you may recall the slew of necessities we already discussed a few chapters back. Lastly, there's general comfort to consider. Here, we can include the 7,001 adorable outfits that baby possesses (each and every one, of course, being a must-have), bibs, burp cloths, diapers, wipes, and pacifiers. Holy crap, guys.

Have you ever seen one of those reality shows that looks into the life of a hoarder? Bathtubs filled with boxes, stack after stack of books, spare rooms jam-packed with who-knows-what from floor to ceiling, and an accumulation of so many things, in general, that there is literally a *path* to get from heap A to heap B[1]? Soooo not me. If there is such a thing as an anti-hoarder, in fact, that's where I fall into line. I despise clutter and the possession of anything that isn't serving a purpose in the worst way. Even thinking about visiting the home of a hoarder is enough to raise my blood pressure and give me a sense of "ugh" in the belly. Before I became a parent, it was easy to keep an orderly home, put things in their place, and avoid the presence of bulky tripping hazards. After baby? Nope. So much *stuff*.

I suspected that life with a newborn was going to be a challenge for anti-clutter me the day of my first baby shower. Cars full of boxes and bags were piled into my living room while I sat by and looked on in amazement and sheer horror. I may have even rubbed my ever-growing bump and whispered something like, "You better be worth this, kiddo!" (and he *was*, of course). Do you remember Old Mother Hubbard? She went to fetch her dog a bone from the cupboard only to find that it was bare? You'll laugh, but my mom used to refer to me as Mother Hubbard for the scarcity of food items in my refrigerator in the era of just Jonathan and I. Back then, I bought food enough only for the week ahead. Discovering that long-lost container of once-moldy, now-petrified lasagna? Not at my house! Well, in the days after bringing Clark home, even my refrigerator was taken over by our new addition. Suddenly, it housed bags and bottles of breastmilk and casseroles enough to feed a small army.

So much of what comes with babies is simply practical, necessary *stuff* for survival. Along with the long list of items mentioned above, this also includes things like bottles of hand sanitizer in every room of the house since touchy-feely visitors can show up anywhere and at any time. There's other *stuff* that newborns introduce into a home too, however. *Stuff* like footprint-adorned documents and the first teeny-tiny cap placed on baby's head at the hospital. Things that I never in a million years would have held onto in my pre-child life: sentimental *stuff*.

I lack sentiment in the worst way. All of my loved ones know this to be true. Although I seriously appreciate (and thrive on, actually) kind words and encouragement from those who matter the most to me, I am not a keeper of handwritten notes, cards, or mementos. If you ever give me a greeting card or a thank you note, I do, in the most sincere way, value what is written. Let it be known, however, that except for on super rare occasions, the second I'm finished reading said note (or the second you leave my house in the event that you've actually handed me the note yourself), it goes in the trash can[2]. My mom has stopped purchasing greeting cards for me for this very reason. On my birthday, she hands me a 20 dollar bill and calls it a day. (Yes, Mom!)

Before Clark, I'll admit that I was a harsh critic of tender folks, like my mother-in-law, who have a hard time parting ways with *stuff*. When I became a parent, though? I got it. Want to hear something hilarious and semi-disturbing all at the same time? I, the individual who has pitched all but maybe two pieces of artwork from her childhood and who immediately tosses away medals and other such awards from the races she participates in, actually had an internal struggle when both Clark and Annie lost their little belly button stumps and had to dispose of the dehydrated, shriveled-up, totally-gross skin (Mom B., I guess I don't have room to talk anymore, do I?!?). Suddenly, it seemed, I went from being the wife whose much-more-sentimental husband has had to adopt the "don't ask, don't tell" policy[3] in order to placate, to being a mom fighting herself to throw away hospital bracelets.

The In-Car Takeover

Even though it was just the two of us at the time and we weren't "*stuff* people", Jonathan and I purchased a large, seven-seater SUV a few years before we had children. The thought was that we were hoping to keep this vehicle for as long as we possibly could and, essentially, run it to the ground. Because of this, we would still have our SUV for several years after having kids, God willing. Even though this did make practical sense to us and we stood behind our decision, there were many times when we wondered to ourselves or to one another whether or not we had gone "too big" and would ever come to a point of actually needing all of the space we had purchased. Well, one not-even-seven-pound baby later, and we already did.

When Clark joined our family, even getting out of the house became a feat, in part because of all of the blasted supplies that would have to go along for the ride. Suddenly, seemingly little decisions, like whether or not to attend a cousin's birthday party at a nearby pizza joint, weren't so little after all. Jonathan and I would have to decide whether or not it was worth it to spend the two years (OK, exaggeration, maybe more like 20 minutes) necessary to think of all of the needed essentials and pack them up in the SUV we were now so thankful for, travel with a baby who would most likely fuss the entire way, and possibly be forced into isolation away from the party anyway should a certain little one decide he was hungry. Car travel with a newborn stinks, period, just because of the mountain of crap you've got to take along... but when you have a baby who defies what everyone else tells you about babies and cars? Extra stinky.

Just like folks told Jonathan and I that having a girl meant being graced with a sweet, calm little being after God gifted us with her feisty, always-moving brother[4], they told us that babies and cars simply went together. I know this certainly *is* true for lots and lots of babes out there, but my two missed out on that memo. Once, when Clark was few days old, the hubs and I attempted getting out for a bit and visited his mom. Albeit tons of hassle to get there, the visit itself went well and Mom B. was tickled pink by our presence. After Clark had finished a breastfeeding session that was just about as successful as he ever managed and seemed to be settling down for a nap, Jonathan and I decided that it was probably a good time to plan our exit. We packed up the SUV with all of our "glorious" *stuff* yet again, got our bambino locked and loaded, bid our farewells, and started the short, 10 to 15 minute trek home.

While I normally sat in the back of the car with Clark in the early days, I had decided to be bold and brave and sit, like a normal adult, in the passenger seat. I got duped. After only a minute or two of travel, I heard a weird, gushing noise and wasn't sure what exactly was going on behind me. I calmly... just kidding... frantically screamed at Jonathan to pull over, which he did. When we opened the door, we discovered our poor babe, his outfit, and basically the entire car seat covered in spit up. To this day, I still don't understand how Clark produced the amount of baby barf he did on that occasion considering how very little he was taking in. Nevertheless, arriving back at home meant a long, tedious cleanup process for Clark and the car seat alike.

Gobs of *stuff* in cars... it sucks. Pools of vomit in cars... it sucks. Know what else totally sucks in a car? Incessant baby cries... something I've grown quite accustomed to in the past three and a half years. A few weeks after Clark's arrival, Jonathan went out with some of his friends for a short time after work. Both of our lives were heavy on the newborn stuff and I thought he could benefit from a brief breather. Since I was hoping for a smooth, enjoyable evening myself, I stopped at the grocery store with Clark quickly to grab a few treats... ice cream and popcorn, of course. The store visit itself wasn't bad. Clark stayed in his car seat, which was perched in the cart, the entire time. He didn't really make a peep. The WHOLE way home, though? Oh, he made lots of peeps. Despite the saving grace that this particular store is close to my house, oh, Mylanta, did that trip ever feel like the longest 10 minutes of my life. Clark screamed, and screamed, and screamed. Naturally, I hit every red light and tried my best to tell Clark we were almost home in a soothing, calm voice. My blood pressure, though, had to have been through the roof. Obviously, we survived, but I promptly stress-ate the crap out of that ice cream the minute I had a chance to grab a spoon. Oh, and believe me when I say that many a pints of ice cream have been eaten in a similar manner following this inaugural event.

While lots of newborns are lulled to sleep by the sounds and motions of moving vehicles, my babies hated car travel from day one. In the Bausman household, crying and car rides just sort of go together, even to this day. And before you judge me for asking for a dual-screen DVD player for my two from their grandparents this past Christmas, try reading "Goodnight Moon" approximately 73 times in a reassuring voice to an inconsolable infant who is tethered in a car seat and wants nothing more than freedom. Just saying…

The Day-to-Day Takeover

If you don't yet have or don't ever plan to have children, I would fathom that many of your daily happenings are rather self-centered. When *you* get in a car, for example, you're not exactly worrying about whether or not you forgot to pack a pacifier or an extra outfit for someone else and you aren't fretting a traffic jam in fear of a backseat driver who may or may not scream at you the entire trip. Your concerns probably look more like whether or not you remembered to grab a thermos of coffee and your cell phone. Oh, and if *you* hit traffic… well, you're nervous about being late or running out of gas. This isn't meant as a dig or with any disrespect to those of you sans minions of the genetic type. It is more an observation, a basic truth, and a recollection of my own kid-free days.

When you've got a child to consider, though, and especially a newborn— the neediest, most-dependent version of a child there is—your thoughts and routines get taken over. *You* are no longer the priority. The priority, now, is the baby, and your thoughts are subject to looking more like:

- "Why are you crying?"
- "How can I get you to stop crying?"

OR

- "What can I do to keep you from crying?"

Some days, becoming a mom felt like someone had placed me on house arrest in a location that had recently gone from clutter-free to "how many babies did you have?!?" in an instant. Instead of following a daily agenda that was created by me with myself as its core focus… my to-do list was dictated by the cries of an infant.

We've touched upon it a few times already, but babies and crying are two things that oftentimes coincide. On a winning day, a baby's cries are quickly quieted with some milk, a pacifier, a cuddle, or an easily-achieved nap. On a losing day, though, we're talking drastic, involved, and sometimes downright ridiculous methods of appeasement. Allowing a little one to nurse, or even just suckle, like allllll day? Yep. Reinserting a rogue pacifier approximately 37 times in order for baby to settle into a nap because the dumb thing keeps popping out? Always. Turning to odd sources of white noise or vibration to simultaneously lull your angel-turned-vigilante and to drown out the mind-numbing wails? Oh, yeah. Personal favorites of ours included the vacuum and the oven fan, while good friends of ours even resorted to popping their kiddo in his car seat atop the dryer (*genius*, Todd and Sue!). The amount of crying a baby does can vary greatly from child to child, but even "easy" babies (I've been told they do exist...) are bound to cry.

When you're accustomed to making independent decisions and creating your own agenda on a day to day basis before becoming a parent, living a life revolving around the cries of a newborn is different and challenging. Even a wee one crying for an obvious, easily-remedied reason, like hunger, is tough... but when a babe's needs are unclear (or unpacifiable as is the case with colic) it can easily become overwhelming! If you strip everything else away, a new parent's entire world essentially involves keeping his or her newborn *from* crying and/or getting his or her newborn to *stop* crying. Just a tad different than pre-baby days, huh?

The Behind-the-Desk Takeover

In case you haven't caught on already (even though I'm pretty sure I'm beating a dead horse by now...), routines and normalcy sort of go out the window when a baby is added to the mix. Pre-baby norms like uncluttered homes, carefree car rides, and self-centered agendas... gone. You know what else is gone, though? Monotonous, yet comfortably predictable workdays. No matter how much time a mom[5] takes away from her "typical" work, stepping back from an office only to be thrown knee-deep (not even close, more like neck-deep) into a life consumed by diapers, sleeplessness, endless feeding cycles and hormonal breakdowns isn't easy.

Besides the obvious differences between traditional work and parenting work, there are other, more subtle things that a new parent may miss... like adult interaction and personal worth. When the visitors fizzle out, it's just you and baby. There aren't any other adult buffers for conversation. Your baby may be the sweetest, cutest-looking thing on the planet, but the level of interaction you're going to get from an infant (or toddler, or child for that matter) just isn't what you're going to get from an adult spouse, partner, colleague, relative, or friend. As much as you may want to hope or pretend that staring at your baby all day long is enough to fuel your human encounter tank, there's a pretty good chance you'll be counting the minutes, some days anyway, until you get to actually speak to someone (ANYONE!?!) who can speak back.

Then, there's the matter of whether or not what you're doing is fulfilling and purposeful like it may have been in the work setting. Even if you don't "like" your job, per se, and are more-than-ready to say sayonara to it for six weeks, twelve weeks, or *indefinitely*, there's still a sense of task-accomplishment and purpose in most paid positions. For me, when life went from administering medications that could have been fatal if dosed incorrectly to counting how many times Clark peed in a 24 hour period and functioning as little more than a milk factory... it was a much harder transition than I had anticipated. Some days, I didn't feel like motherhood looked good on me, or really even worked for me. Some days, there wasn't much, if any, glory in what I was doing, and it certainly didn't leave me feeling accomplished or fulfilled.

Whether it be your house, your car, your daily life, or your work life, bringing home an infant alters it all. Babies introduce *stuff* into our homes that never existed before, they revamp the way we travel, and they completely usurp our priorities. The bad news is that these changes aren't always easy, fun, or welcomed with open arms. Real life? All of these shifts kind of suck to a degree, and some days it would be much easier to hide in a closet with a half dozen donuts than to change one more diaper, listen to one more minute of crying, or walk one more time across the living-room-turned-obstacle-course. Oh, and watching your "other" pull out of the driveway in a quiet, kidless car to head into work where he or she will be able to interact with other adults and maybe perform tasks a tad more meaningful to society than washing poop-stained laundry? It can be downright trying.

So where is the good news in all of this change? Well, while the *stuff* can certainly be overwhelming, most of it is transient[6]. If you're a pregnant first-timer, you'll be amazed at just how quickly many of the baby items you purchased yourself or received as gifts become obsolete and can be put into storage or given away. There will be outfits that are worn once or twice, if ever. And the swings and bouncers and so on? *Some* of them, baby won't take a liking to, and *all* of them he or she will rapidly outgrow.

As far as the difficult, let's-pray-we-make-it-in-one-piece-and-with-our-sanity-intact car rides? They get a tad easier as you grow to learn your baby and all of his or her cues, routines, likes, and dislikes. I know that when you're in the thick of the newborn days, toddlerhood seems like something that is a million miles away. Rest assured that before you know it, however, that tiny, car-despising, little one of yours will be a fully-bribable child. When your *toddler* is having a rough go of a car ride or when Mom is at her wits' end? Toss that kiddo some crackers, a sippy cup, a book, an obnoxiously loud toy, or… let's get real because I do it all the time… even a bag full of candy for flip's sake.

While I won't say that listening to crying necessarily ever becomes easy, I will say that it becomes a new norm and is at least easi*er*. With every passing day, you and your sweetie will grow more tightly bonded and signals for specific needs will become more identifiable to you. You'll know your baby's hungry cry versus her tired cry sooner than you think. And on those occasions like the night(s) Clark wailed for hours on end without apparent reason? The times you have no idea *what* is wrong and how you can fix it? Well, you'll learn that you are more resilient than you know, that you can function on far less sleep than you've ever imagined, and, if you're like me, that husbands and Jesus are made for calling upon.

Ultimately, work will return, if and when you want or need it to. The predictability of a workday? You can get it back. You know what you *can't* get back? These fleeting, tiny-baby moments. Yes, there's lots of change, and sacrifice, and even struggle when a child is born… but there's lots of good and beautiful stuff too that is very, very temporary. Gone are the days, guys. Gone are the days of babies napping peacefully on my chest. Gone are the days when I, or something I had produced, was all my little one needed for nourishment. Gone, too, are the days when my child was immune to "big" feelings like jealousy, worry, or loss. While there are certainly things that I'm glad to see gone… like long days (and nights) of infant cries… there are also things I miss. The reflex of a smile that would light up Clark's face as he *finally* slumbered in my arms after puddles of tears, for example? Well, those smiles were enough to renew my soul for another day of parenthood, were far more weighty than my exhaustion, and were far more important than the at-home, in-car, or at-work lifestyles I had traded in for this new assignment.

---

1. During our last pancake-inhaling session at IHOP—just in case you care my favorite variety is the chocolate, chocolate chip because, duh, *chocolate*—my cousin, Missy, told Alicia and I of her recent experience with hoarding. For a few months, Missy had been paid to provide assistance to an elderly woman who had fallen into hoarding after the death of her husband. Everything I described was exactly what Missy encountered in this home. One of her paid tasks was actually to help un-stack, organize, and re-stack mounds of unneeded books.

2. I think Annie speaks my love language. One of her favorite phrases right now is "throw away!" Ha.

3. When Jonathan sees yet another garbage bag full of items at the curb, he doesn't even ask what's inside anymore to save himself from feeling a loss of any sort. I'm kind of the worst.

4. Nope, not at all—this girl is SASSY and busy, busy, busy,,,

5. Oh dud! After Clark was born, I had a mere six weeks at home with my precious little guy. Because I hadn't been with my workplace for 12 months, I didn't yet qualify for a full leave under the Family Medical Leave Act of 1993 (FMLA). Thankfully, Jonathan had a lot of personal time accrued with his employer, and when I returned unwillingly to work, he was able to stay at home with Clark for another nine weeks. I can't even express to you how grateful I am to have a husband who not only was able to do this, but intensely *wanted* to. It made the shift from home to work much easier for me to swallow, and it gave Jonathan time with Clark that he will always treasure. When Jonathan had to return to work, guys, I was a MESS. Even taking Clark to my sister, who I adore and trust completely, tore my heart out. I was in such an awful emotional state the first morning we had to drop off our babe that Jonathan very literally had to give me step by step instructions on how to dress myself. Real life.

6. ...and all the anti-hoarders of the world say a collective HALLELUJAH! Except, don't get too excited guys, because the baby *stuff* is just replaced with toddler *stuff*, which is replaced by big-kid *stuff*. Sigh...

9 ONE PLUS ONE EQUALS THREE

When I met Jonathan, he was a measly 12 years old and I, a modest 14. We were young and naive and had absolutely no idea what the future would hold for us. While it's true that I asked my father-in-law for permission to marry his son repeatedly not too long after we'd met, it was (mostly) in jest, and it's completely surreal to sit back and reflect on the fact that our lives converged. To imagine Jonathan as my husband, for *real*, would have been crazy enough in those days... but to imagine he and I together parenting two babies in tandem? Bonkers!

Jonathan and I met at church and were blessed to spend a lot of our formative years growing up together in a tight-knit group of friends. Long, long before we were ever a couple, we ate together, we laughed together, we served together, we traveled together, we prayed together, and we learned together. Pretty cool. There was always a sort of chemical attraction between the two of us[1], but our chances at anything real seemed unlikely... for multiple reasons. Namely, I was over two and a half years Jonathan's senior. In the grand scheme of the world, two and a half years is nothing, I know, and we laugh about it ever mattering, now. When you're in high school, though, and you've got a crush on a middle schooler? Totally a big deal.

As the years passed, our friendship deepened, and our surface-level feelings grew into something more substantial, though, an age difference started mattering *less* as I started desiring Jonathan *more*. It was becoming evident to the both of us where things were headed, so it was at this time that I gave my future man two stipulations if he wanted to date me. For starters, he needed to be taller than I was (as if this was in his control). For finishers (?), since it was already half-embarrassing that I, as a college freshman, was considering a relationship with a high school student, he at least needed to be able to drive a car without a parent in the passenger seat. Requirement number one? My hubby isn't a tall guy by any means, but at 5'6", he's taller than me. Requirement number two? Well, basically the day after Jonathan had a driver's license in his back pocket and my second stipulation was met, he and I had our first "official" date. The rest is history.

Jonathan and I dated for a few years and married, practically, as babies. At the ripe old ages of 20 and 22, my sweet husband wasn't even old enough to have a celebratory toast at his own wedding. Sparkling grape juice, anyone? We were young, and there were definitely those who thought that perhaps we still had some life that needed living before settling down into marriage. Despite this, I have never (ever, ever) once regretted making this man my husband when I did. I've said it before, and I'll say it again. Jonathan is my *person*. He knows the ugliest parts of me and the best parts of me. He knows how to read my nonsense and balance me. While I am quick to question, and analyze, and find fault in things… even, sadly, the things that he says and does sometimes… he always encourages and uplifts me.

You want to know what Jonathan did when I told him I wanted to try my hand at writing a book? He drove an hour both ways after working a full day to go pick up a laptop that he bought for me so that I could go for it and get started. Not even just a run-of-the-mill, basic, cheap laptop either. Jonathan wanted me to have something lasting and of quality. If he had proposed the same thing to me? I'd like to think that I, too, would have supported his dreams and been the wind beneath his wings… but I'll be real with you on this one. I probably would have rolled my eyes or been semi-on-board and semi-skeptical at the same time.

Just last night, in fact, Jonathan mentioned something about the prospect of earning a little extra money each month by (Nerd Alert) "mining" Ethereum. If you, like me, have absolutely no idea nor any desire to know what this means, just understand that it's basically a techie way of setting up computers to build (…or find? Who knows/cares…haha!) electronic currency that can be sold for actual cash. Weird, right? Well, anyway, this sort of thing is right up Jonathan's alley and is something that I'm sure he could be successful with. He is capable of teaching himself anything[2], and he *loves* to learn, like almost obsessively[3]. It's simultaneously one of the coolest and most annoying things about my husband.

I know it might sound a little crazy or impossible, but I have been sitting here mulling it over for quite a while now, and I honest-to-goodness cannot think of a single time since becoming Jonathan's "other" that I have ever felt judged or criticized by him. Me, on the other hand? I'm critical *always*, and it's something I am very far from proud of. When Jonathan made mention of his thoughts about Ethereum last night, for example, my reaction was much different than his was when I shared the idea of writing a book. Think along the lines of less supportive and more "seriously?" My husband isn't a saint, and yes of course he has flaws too... but I am big time blessed with this guy, and I *know* it.

Before having Clark, Jonathan and I were married for over five years and made a point of doing and seeing a lot, together. As far as the "big" things, we ventured to Hawaii, California, Mexico, Texas, and Greece. As far as the "little", we have always enjoyed food of all sorts, and it wasn't uncommon for us to plan mini-outings where we'd grab takeout or to dine out as a couple every few days. We ran together, we wasted many an hour binge-watching all of "Lost" in the earliest days of binge-watching, we rented movies like two and three times a week, and we drank *hot* coffee... *simultaneously* (the glory days!). I remember thinking that our lives were busy and wishing for more time even then. Oh, how very clueless I was. How on Earth we filled an entire evening without having two tiny people to chase around, feed, wipe, bathe, entertain, clean up after, and get ready for bed (which is like a 20 to 30 minute process in and of itself)? Who knows!

Every aspect of my marriage changed when the Bausman family transitioned from a party of two to a party of three. Even before Clark arrived, things were different. Meal planning and prep is my forte and something I really enjoy, but in those early days of pregnancy when morning (or not... try *all* day) sickness and food aversions prevailed? I was useless. I was a grad student at the time, so tired, and so sick, and can very literally remember an evening when I was sitting in the kitchen with my head on the table, in tears because of the hour-long commute and three-hour-long class that awaited me.

To make this image even more comical, I was also forcing a bowl of Cinnamon Toast Crunch down my throat because simple, terrible-for-you, carbs were all I could even fathom introducing to my stomach. I looked at Jonathan and said, "I have no idea what to even tell you to eat, but you're going to have to figure it out on your own." Well, figure it out he did. Jonathan and I survived those terrible, early days of pregnancy both times around. He, with lots of takeout, and I with hard candy and small amounts of carbs around the clock for weeks.

Pregnancy days were different enough, but when Clark made his grand entrance? Nothing looked the same. My body was different. My thoughts were different. My routine was different. My home was different. And my marriage? Well... *different*. My world, and our world as a couple, was Clark. My own needs were tossed to the sidelines... I barely had time to pee or shower those first couple of never-ending days... and Jonathan's? It would be a lie to pretend that I even acknowledged or, let's be honest, cared what he needed. *I* was the one who carried around this little load for 39 long weeks. *I* was the one whose body was stretched, and split, and swollen, and sore. *I* was the one who this little guy depended upon for nourishment. Jonathan? What had *Jonathan* done? I almost dared him to tell me that he was tired. Isn't that plain awful?

I know it's totally unkind and selfish that I felt this way when it's not like Jonathan had a say in the matter in any way. We didn't exactly get to choose which of us would be pregnant, give birth, or breastfeed. Further, it's not like he didn't do everything he could do to help me and care for our baby. Jonathan changed diapers, washed pump parts and bottles, and shushed our fussy infant overnight because he *wanted* to and because he was willing to lighten my load in whatever way possible. I know this now, and I knew it then, but quite frankly it didn't change the way I felt. Becoming a parent and having so much of the burden fall on my shoulders created in me this underlying sense of resentment that I hadn't experienced before. If and when he did tell me that he was tired? Jonathan got the look of all looks and was darned lucky he never suffered any bodily harm (Kidding! Sort of.).

In the early days of Clark, one of the biggest changes for us as a couple was simply the preparation and effort that had to go into even *thinking* about leaving the house. You all know I'm a planner, we've already established that as fact, but any and all tiny bits of spontaneity that I may have possessed pre-baby were super gone the second I became a mother. Before we had kids, if Jonathan and I wanted to rent a movie on a weeknight, or go out for ice cream after dinner, or take a walk around the neighborhood because it was a nice day outside, we just did it without a second thought. As new parents, though, these things just weren't going to happen unless we really, *really* thought them through.

A movie on a weeknight, or ever? Yeah, right. We would either fall asleep or have to pause it 700 times. Go out for ice cream? Uhh, do we really want to exposure ourselves to germy tables and coughing people? No, thanks. Take a walk? Hmm. Sounds easy enough. OK! Let's do it. And then came the flurry of preparative activities:

1. Change baby's diaper
2. Add layers of clothing to baby for warmth
3. Find a pacifier
4. Grab a blanket
5. Hunt down a rattle
6. Hear something come from baby's Southern regions
7. Change baby's diaper again to discover a full-fledged blowout
8. Dig through every drawer for another outfit
9. Clothe baby once more
10. Head out to the stroller in the garage
11. Properly secure baby in the stroller
12. Open the garage to discover that it's already dark outside
13. Try again tomorrow (raining).
14. Try again the next day (too cold).
15. The next? (Ah, screw it.)
16. Stay at home and inside forever.

Ultimately, Jonathan, Clark, and I were kept rather cooped up in our first days as a family of three. On top of suffering from Cabin Fever, Jonathan and I were majorly sleep deprived (shocking, right?) and in some ways grieving over the loss of our former life as a married couple. While we *love-*loved Clark, there was some notable tension between the two of us as we adjusted and worked to rediscover our groove. Every decision that we made, either independently or as a couple, suddenly revolved around our brand-new baby. I mean… *every*.

You'll laugh, but there were times when Jonathan or I would be holding a conked-out little Clark on the couch when even going to the bathroom was tantamount to treason. If we laid him down? Nap time was over. What are the options when you've got an ultra-full bladder and are cradling a napping newborn?

1. Uncomfortably (OK—downright painfully) hold said pee until baby wakes

2. Somehow figure out how to pee while holding baby without waking baby

3. Give up on either of the above options, lay baby down, run to the bathroom to relieve yourself, and return to find your cranky wife now awake from her *own* nap and bouncing a crying baby. The death stare says it all…

I remember treating Jonathan like a bitty-bladdered preschooler on more than one occasion and double checking to make sure that he used the bathroom before settling Clark into a nap on the couch. It's just hilarious that using the toilet suddenly became a "luxury" post baby. Clark's influence on our life didn't end in the bathroom, though. It stretched to the kitchen.

Even food, something that both Jonathan and I fully enjoy— more than almost anything else in life, in fact[4]— was wrapped up in our infant. To the collective "Amen" of every parent ever, it felt like any time we attempted to eat in those first days, there would be a blip. We so very quickly came to realize that peaceful meals were a part of our past. Inevitably, the second our meal would be ready, Clark would wake from a sound sleep crying, I'd look at the clock and realize that I had forgotten to pump, an unexpected visitor would show up at the door, or I'd find myself in one of my irrational and unpredictable confrontations with the Evil Evening. At that point, we'd either be forced to inhale our food at lightning speed[5], take turns eating, or do what needed to be done and return later to cold food.

On top of this, we discovered that even *what* we ate as new parents was dictated by our child. If something crossed my lips that our babe's digestive system wasn't keen on, Jonathan and I both paid for it later. Big time. Clark's belly and fiber-dense foods, like beans, never mixed well. For Annie, it was anything fried. I rarely ever eat fried food, thankfully, but on the off chance that I'd forget about our girl's sensitivity and (I swear) eat a single one of Daddy's french fries from Chick-Fil-A? Our normally even-keeled sweetie would *scream*.

Prior to children, an evening after work for Jonathan and I looked a lot like us sitting down to dinner together, unwinding in front of the television, and chatting about our days. I typically returned home about an hour or so before he did, and I *enjoyed* this little bit of quiet time to myself. It was a nice chance for me to get comfortable and shift gears from work life to home life while prepping for dinner. Truly, it was a form of catharsis. As a new parent, though, while I had lots of time at home without Jonathan, it wasn't the relaxing, peaceful, quiet, or cathartic time I was accustomed to. Suddenly, I found myself looking at the clock... like every five minutes... to see if it was time for him to come back yet. I missed him. I missed adult connection. I missed an extra set of hands to help with feedings, and washing pump parts, and changing diapers, and bouncing a fussy baby.

And when he did make it home? Well, there wasn't a relaxed pace to our evenings together, at all. Instead, Jonathan got "dumped" on. He'd get dumped on with word vomit as I'd relay all of the baby happenings—good and bad—of the day. He'd get dumped on with responsibilities because I both wanted and needed a break. He'd get dumped on with the wails of an infant as evenings were always the fussiest times for our two. And... he'd often get dumped on with my own hormonal, exhausted tears as I continued to adapt and adjust to something completely different and new... remember the Evil Evening?

No part of our marriage looked quite the same after Jonathan and I became parents. Even, and especially, our sex life (... you didn't really think I'd be able to omit a sex talk, did you?). My *attraction* to this man never wavered in those early days. In all truth, it may have even been deepened. I adored Jonathan all the more for giving me the precious gift of a child and I treasured watching him become the Daddy I knew he would be. Physical needs and desires though? Well, they just had a way of taking a backseat to fatigue and task accomplishment. Clark needed to eat. I needed to pump. A diaper needed to be changed. We all needed (in the worst way) to sleep. Sex, although desirable, wasn't absolutely *needed*... so, sometimes, it waited in the wings.

Simply stated, the relationship between Jonathan and I shifted. In our deepest, real-est time of adjustment and sleep deprivation, we found ourselves needing each other less for companionship, fulfillment, and for pleasure than we had previously been accustomed to in our marriage. What we needed each other for then, it seemed, was backup and support. If you had wire-tapped our house in those days, you would have heard lots of things like...

- "Love, can you grab me another pack of wipes?"
- "When did Clark last eat?"
- "Have you seen a nunny (what we called a pacifier) anywhere?"

OR

- "Hey, can you please start warming a bottle for me?"

OK... and maybe some of these things too..

- "Did *we* eat anything today?"
- "Can you please hold him for like 5 minutes so I can actually take a shower?"
- "If I have to wash another pump part, I'm going to shoot somebody."

OR

- "I just want to sleeeeeeeeeeeeeep."

We kind of looked and felt more like teammates or coworkers in those days than intimate spouses. Truly, we were just trying to lend each other a hand, do whatever needed to be done, and survive the day. We needed one another, don't get me wrong, it just wasn't for all of the same reasons we had needed each other for before having children.

Eventually, we adapted to a life of perpetual tiredness, and sex started to look both more appealing and feasible. Even then, however, it was entirely different. For starters, my post-baby body was in no way, shape, or form similar to the body I inhabited prior to gestation. I know I'm getting eye-rolls here because I told you that I hadn't gained much weight during my pregnancy with Clark and have a thinner build than many, in general, but I'm not really talking about things on the outside, guys. Delivery sort of wrecked me... internally. Do you remember the adhesion we discussed several chapters ago when I divulged the gross, dripping tales of my recovering-from-childbirth days? Well, guess what? Somehow, that was just the tip of the iceberg. Not too long after my six week visit, there was even *more* fun down below.

In case you weren't aware, when a baby is born vaginally, the best case scenario is that he or she is facing downwards, towards the mother's bottom. Sometimes, babies will present themselves in the opposite fashion, and this is referred to as being "sunny side up". Well, true to form in every way, Clark followed neither of these routes and forged his own method of entry into the world. He, instead, decided to be born facing my hip in a "transverse" position. While I exited delivery fairly unscathed, initially, with only a first degree tear and a small laceration (layman's terms translation: I had some minor damage to the skin in my lady regions from stretching), there were other, latent problems that emerged as time passed.

A few weeks after my first follow up, I very literally had parts of me bulging out of my nethers. Not only was I the winner of a vaginal adhesion, but I also scored a prolapsed bladder and bowel in the process of delivery. Basically, the tissues that normally support these organs were stretched and stressed to the point that they no longer had the holding strength they once did. End result? I've got droopy things in my pelvis[6].

In case you also weren't aware, sometimes, a pregnancy can actually cause a women's abdominal muscles to separate, known as diastasis recti. This is a fairly common occurrence, and is something that most often resolves on its own in the months following delivery. In some cases, however, the stretching is more severe and will likely never heal without physical therapy or surgical correction. Well, right on trend, guess whose belly wall still resembles a 7-10 split? To this day, when I lay on the floor and use what remains of my core muscles to assume the position of a sit-up, you can legitimately insert a few fingers directly through my abdomen.

In case you also-*also* weren't aware (ha, sorry), breastfeeding boobs don't just let down for babies. Oh, no. They are touchy little devils who may very well let down for your husband. They are so spiteful, in fact, that they might let down simply because you are thinking about the fact that they might let down and are doing your best to focus on having sex instead of willing your girls to behave. If you know me personally and want to be able to look me in the face without turning red in embarrassment ever again, I totally give you permission to stop reading now, but here come some visuals. While breastfeeding, if Jonathan and I attempted sex topless, he got squirted. If we attempted sex partially clothed, I would either leak through my nursing pads or become engorged and sore. Often times, this resulted in us "planning" sex around both nap times and pump times. How *completely* sexy.

So I had lady regions containing normally-not-there organs, a belly that was basically split down the middle, and breastfeeding boobs that could blow at any moment. Add to all of this nonsense the basic fact that I was self-conscious about my post-baby body, in general, and the idea that my husband may see me in a new light after birthing a baby? You can imagine why sex was just a little different for Jonathan and I in the post baby days.

What's more? Post-baby days included...duh... a baby. Yes, there was a baby in the house and usually within five feet of Jonathan and I— at all times. We both knew that it wasn't like Clark was going to process any of what was going down or even be aware that something was happening, but it still took a little bit of adjustment to get past a certain "ick factor" of often having an audience. Quite simply, it just felt kind of weird or wrong.

Transitioning from two to three (and then four) changed our entire world, and our marriage certainly wasn't exempt. Some things we expected, like sleep deprivation, and other things... like sex becoming a spectator sport... not so much. Before motherhood, I would have told you that having children wouldn't change my love for Jonathan, but honestly, it did. It didn't change it in *bad* ways, don't get me wrong, but it did change it. If you've yet to experience parenthood firsthand and have a baby on the way, change is coming. The love you have and feel for your "other"? It's going to change.

Since babies have been added to the mix, my love for Jonathan has become broader and deeper. It goes far, far beyond physical needs, surface-level attraction, and even companionship. Those things are still present and important (although sometimes hidden by the demands of a life with children, if I'm being honest), but they're coupled now with a love that is lots-of-times *practical*. In the newborn days, we had a relationship that often looked like serving the other as an extra set of hands for changing diapers, scrubbing spit up stains, and washing pump parts for the 17th time in one day. Today, it's serving as a second set of hands to keep two toddlers from running into the street, scrubbing glitter glue from little fingers, and washing the kitchen floor for the 17th time in one day because far less food ends up in a toddler's stomach during mealtime than you can imagine.

It's OK to need your partner for different reasons after a baby. It's OK to love him or her differently, too. The key? Adjust *together*. When you're tired (you will be), and hormonal (you will be), and just *over* all of the newborn stuff you didn't expect (you super will be)… fall apart together. Speak from an honest place with one another, even if what you say is kind of ugly or selfish. Acknowledge that nothing looks the same. Try praying together or *for* your "other". And even though it's hard? Get out together. As soon as you are able to, utilize those grandparents who are chomping at the bit to get their hands on your little one, and *get out of the house together*. Even for like an hour. Guys, you know my control-freak ways and my crazy levels of attachment to Clark and Annie. Leaving tiny ones in the care of others, even *trusted* others, is hard. It will take some planning, some ironing out of details, and some self-motivation, but you will be a better parent for finding and making time for your other half. I promise.

I have been blessed to call Jonathan my husband for almost nine years now. There has never been a single moment in that time when I have doubted or regretted the decision to couple my life with his. He isn't perfect, and I sure as heck am far from it, but I am so thankful for "us". As I sit here typing this, it's just me, my thoughts, my laptop, and my caramel macchiato… made possible because my sweet man offered me an evening to myself. He, meanwhile, is very literally wrangling our two in the bathroom next door and giving them baths. Marriage, especially when you are parents together, is about far more than intimacy. Sometimes, it's about keeping little bellies full, keeping little bottoms clean, and keeping little bodies clothed… together.

1. One of our friends, on multiple occasions, made comments to us like… "Would you two just date and get it over with?" Miss you, Mikey!

2. Among the many things Jonathan has taught himself, some of the most notable are playing guitar and photography. He has also tackled a million household projects with no prior knowledge of the task at hand, simply by watching YouTube videos. He's kind of awesome.

3. Any decision that is ever made in our home is backed by meticulous research, so I never have to worry whether or not big decisions are the "right" decision. Remember those windows we just purchased? Well, Jonathan legitimately created spreadsheets comparing the specs of several window models sold by local companies. If you've ever got a window question, maybe just ask my husband first. While some folks stay up late watching sitcoms, Jonathan watches product reviews for mattresses. Real life.

4. We love food and drink to an almost-unhealthy level. Every month, Jonathan and I each allow ourselves a bit of "kitty" money. This is a designated amount of funds that we have built into our budget which falls outside of all of the *necessary* things, like groceries, fuel, utilities, mortgage, diapers, etc. Our sacred kitty money is just that… *our* money… for he and I to spend independently, on whatever, whenever, and without (much) consideration of the other three members of the family. In a typical month, the majority of *my* kitty money is spent on specialty food and drinks like fancy popcorn, clean "sodas", and stevia-sweetened ice cream. *Jonathan's* is usually top-shelf Scotch, olives, quality cheeses, sushi, or the ever-classy order of hot wings (which, much to his dismay, our children have taken a strong liking to in recent weeks… I predict many a 9PM takeout orders in our future). We spend on other things, too, but food always, always tops the list.

5. I Hate (with a capital H), eating food quickly. For me, it's like taking one of the simplest pleasures in life—good food—and stripping away its luster. My sisters and husband will tell you that this is 600% true, but I am actually known to take dessert from family gatherings "to-go", so that I can savor them once my never-still toddlers are in bed and asleep for the evening. I do this on my side of the family, anyway. Jonathan's family hasn't quite caught on yet to how crazy I am. Ha!

6. Thankfully, with time and some suggestions of my OB/GYN, all of this has gotten better to a degree. I still (sort of) jokingly say that Clark turned my body inside out when he made his exit.

WRAP UP

If becoming a parent and bringing home two newborns less than two years apart has been nothing else, it's been quite a ride. A flight, to be more exact. Some days, the journey has been smooth, and exciting, and provided me with a view of the sun and clouds that I wasn't capable of seeing from the ground. Some days, though, the ride has been a turbulent red-eye that left me with ears that wouldn't pop and the mother of all jet lags. There have been moments of joy and love and wonder and growth and celebration and cheers and hilarity along the way... but there have also been lots of moments of disappointment and guilt and shock and fatigue and frustration and sadness and stress and even isolation. Beyond a doubt, becoming a parent brought to my life all of the good things that I had hoped it would. It just *also* happened to bring along a bunch of not-so-good things that I had never even fathomed.

Ultimately, I hope that reading this book has been a little bit for you like the introduction to parenthood has been for me. I hope that while it brought us to places of candor, and ugliness, and several doses of reality, it may also have been a source of laughter, a reminder that the most beautiful things in life are often the weightiest, and an illustration of the truth that more unites us as parents and humans than separates us. Thank you for coming along with me, thank you for bearing with me, and thank you for maybe trying to keep a straight face the next time our paths cross and all you can picture is me squirting my husband with breast milk.

As our time together comes to an end, let's take a few moments to reflect on the "big picture points" we've discussed.

Real-Life Thoughts

For starters, although friends and family will give you all kinds of advice and wisdom (whether you seek it out or not), lots of the *messy* and *awful* details will be left out. When you find yourself thinking some terrible, unfiltered, very non-rainbow things about parenthood in general or the crap-tastic day you're having as a new mom or dad, just know that you're not alone. In the newborn days (and many, many days since), I thought quite a few flat-out-horrible things that I never would have foreseen myself thinking… and, you know what? I still think I'm a pretty good mom. *Most* of the time, anyway.

Real-Life Bodies

Next, we discussed the realities of a body after birth. Labor is hard and traumatic, and even when it goes well and as planned, it'll still leave your body in shambles. While the experience of childbirth may look vastly different from one woman to the next, it's after effects? Not so much. You'll be sore, tired, dripping, and forever different regardless of what medications were or were not used, how long it took baby to get here, and by what route he or she arrived. My thoughts on this one? Anticipate and expect the mess, celebrate your body for the job it's done, and restrain yourself from screaming (or passing out) the first time you take a peek down yonder after your melon makes its debut (TMI? Sorry!).

Real-Life Fatigue

Then, there's being exhausted like you've never been exhausted in all of your life. Until you've been there yourself, the fatigue experienced after bringing home a newborn is really unimaginable. Babies may sleep *often*, but they don't necessarily sleep *a lot* as is commonly assumed. Because of this, it's no surprise that new parents lack in the sleep department and look a little rough around the edges for quite some time when their family grows. On this subject, I challenge you to accept help from others in whatever way or ways work best for you and your crew, lean on and communicate with your spouse or closest support person like you never have before, and, *yes*… as much as is (im)*possible*... "sleep when baby sleeps". Truthfully, this might look like a few short, scattered naps for Mom... both day *and* night...sigh...

Real-Life Feedings

Next up to bat? Breastfeeding. The "easiest" and most "natural" way to feed your baby.... or something like that. When it doesn't come super easy, as was the case both times around for me, breastfeeding is clumsy at best and so challenging in the beginning. Even for those who have simpler experiences than I had, making the choice to breastfeed an infant and actually carrying out that decision is a huge, huge commitment. What's our favorite F-word when it comes to feedings? You should know it by now—FREQUENT. Frequent feedings may be precious and tender and special in many ways, but I'm just going to say it, guys, they kind of suck, too. And in the beginning? They take *forever*. Like practically long enough to get you to the next feeding. Whatever method of feeding you settle upon, I pray you can do so with peace and with your head held high. No matter the source, keeping a baby nourished is demanding, and it's one of the most important jobs for new parents! Set the bar low. Gear up to feed your baby a million times a day. Fully expect discomfort and frustration and even some struggle, too. Why? Because then, when it "clicks" even for a second, when you see that this tiny being that you made is thriving because of your efforts... it feels amazing. Or when the teeny fingers on that perfect, little hand wrap around your own? There's *nothing* better. Nothing.

Real-Life Emotions

After this, we ventured together into the world of crying. When hormones strike (or vanish) and you're in a constant state of fatigue, it's only natural to cry... and cry you will (and will, and will, and will). Both times around, I cried about *everything* those first days even though crying isn't something I do much on "typical" terms. To an onlooker, I'm sure sometimes I looked hilarious, sometimes frightening, and sometimes heart-wrenching. Anticipate the tears. Tell yourself now that no matter how much of a crier you are or are not, tears will find you and they'll make you feel a few parts crazy and a few parts silly more than once. Also... maybe play the "For How Many Consecutive Days Will _____ Lose It" game with your hubs. It's kind of fun.

Real-Life Drop-Ins

Next in line was the super-touchy topic of visitors. I won't lie, I've got a few unresolved butterflies in the belly about this chapter going public because I'm a little afraid of hurting some feelings. Nevertheless, I kept it real because the honest truth is that even visits from your closest loved ones can be both so stressful and so welcomed at the same time in the newborn days. In many ways, be it by the gift of food, help around the house, or just an extra set of (rested, non-hormonal) hands to hold a fussy baby, guests make life for new parents easier. In a few other ways, however, those same guests can make life awkward and taxing. When you're a brand-new parent who is still trying to figure out how to survive the demands of a baby... feeding schedules, sleeping schedules, and visitor schedules are, simply, a lot to juggle. How, then, can these visits be the most helpful and beneficial to both the visitor and the visited? I say it's about open and honest communication, flexibility, and throwing any and all expectations of a quiet, peaceful, fluid visit out the closest window. Enjoy your guests, parents! They'll be missed soon enough.

Real-Life Demons

Additionally, we uncovered the mystery that is the Evil Evening. As dusk approaches, loved ones return home from work, distractions are lessened, and the cries of babes are unleashed to their full potential, it's no wonder that many new moms struggle to maintain composure during these unsettling, kind-of-scary hours. When you're sitting down to dinner one evening and burst into a mess of tears for no good reason at all other than you couldn't help it, remember that you are not alone. Chuckle at yourself (in retrospect, at least), like I did, and shrug it off. This nonsense doesn't last forever. Sleep will come again. Routines will come again. Your sanity? It will too, I promise!

Real-Life Shake-Ups

And then, we took a hard look at how newborns change lives. *Every* aspect of lives. Whether it be how a home physically looks and functions, how a person travels from Point A to Point B, how decisions are made and tasks are prioritized, or how "work" is perceived and/or completed, it's all fair game. Believe me when I say that not a single aspect of one's daily, pre-child life is immune to the effects of bringing home a newborn. Your orderly, clutter-free family room? Your uninterrupted, quiet car ride? Your "me focused", self-created agenda? Your predictable, accomplishment-driven work day? Gone, gone, gone, and… gone. How does a parent cope, then, with all of this change when it is often overwhelming, tiring, and challenging? Remember that the *stuff* is temporary, that infants turn into toddlers who are much more bribable in cars, that putting your child's needs before your own will be willingly ingrained into your being before you think possible, and that, unlike the finite newness and tiny-ness of your sweet newborn which you can't get back, work will return if and when you want or need it to.

Real-Life Marriages

Lastly, we analyzed the shifts in committed relationships that are inevitable when a couple transitions into a family. Even before a baby is born, pregnancy days will bring changes to a partnership due to their hormone surges, nausea, and relentless exhaustion. When an infant arrives on the scene, however? More will look different, to be honest, than the same between spouses. Roles will be different. Routines will be different. Needs will be different. Schedules will be different. Basic decision making will be different. And sex, of course, will be different. If you find yourselves in a position similar to Jonathan and I, you and your "other" will need each other less for intimacy and companionship and more for tactical support in the earliest of newborn days. Especially if you're a new mom who is still split, swollen, and sore… you may even find yourself with a newfound sense of envy or resentment towards your other half. So what is the secret to success here? How can a couple survive and thrive during such a demanding and depleting time of drastic change? Communicate. Adjust together. Fail together. Grow together. Mourn the loss of your old lives and those coveted, sleep-filled nights of long ago together. Pray for one another. Support one another. And when you spot yet another pile of unwashed pump parts in the sink… serve one another, and start washing.

I hope you've laughed with me as you've turned (or clicked) through the pages and chapters of this book. I hope, especially for the pregnant readers and partners, that my realities, my recollections, and my honesty haven't left you feeling scared and questioning whether or not parenthood was a good decision. I hope, instead, that I leave you feeling informed. I hope that I leave you stockpiled with a slew of my own silly absurdities enough to help you feel less crazy when you find yourself in similar shoes very soon. I hope that I leave you empowered enough to cherish the wonder and all of the beautiful bits of bringing home a baby... because when you're tired, hormonal, and residing in a post-delivery body that is basically ramshackled, it's easy for the precious moments to get lost in the shuffle.

My best advice? Acknowledge the wreck you (and most likely your partner) are. Feel what you feel, talk to whoever will listen, and refuse to isolate yourself in ugly, guilt-ridden thoughts. If you're thinking it, chances are I, and *loads* of other new parents, do... or did... too. Before we become parents, it's easy to think that life with a newborn will be far more rewarding than it is depleting. Real life, though, guys? Not always. While being blessed with children is, *ultimately*, the greatest gift I've ever been given, I'll be honest here and say that the vast majority of the time, I hit my bed at night feeling as though I've given far more as a mom than I've gotten back. I wouldn't trade it for the world, don't get me wrong, but my expectations of parenthood in comparison to what it truly is now, and was in the newborn stage? Very different. That gross feeling of disappointment so many new parents either openly or secretly feel when the cupcakes of their anticipation taste more like communion wafers in reality? Weltschmerz. It's no surprise that so many of us as new parents experience Weltschmerz, especially when we don't openly talk about the less-than-perfect parts of parenthood as much as we should.

Now that you've read this book, *my* silence has officially come to an end. You now know far more about almost every part of my body than you ever could have desired (sorry again to those of you who actually *know* me...) and have gotten a look at some of the rawest and most private thoughts and experiences I've ever had. Why? Because I really feel that shining light on some of these situations and reflecting on them with the ability to laugh at myself openly is freeing, not only to me, but to other new moms and new dads out there who have, or will have, similar struggles. It's in recognizing, accepting, and sometimes sharing the parts of parenting I struggle with that allow me to savor and enjoy the parts that I love. Newborns are the worst, it's true, but they're also the best. If you're reading this and you've got a baby in the works: Get ready for the chest to chest snuggles. Get ready for the itty-bitty toes. Get ready for the cutest sleep-noises ever. Get ready for deep,

deep, deep, deep love. Get ready. Although lots of heavy, hard stuff is on the way... these *wonderful* things are coming too!

WOULD YOU DO ME A FAVOR?

If you enjoyed coming along on this hormone-filled ride with me (or even if you didn't), hop on over to Amazon and leave a short, honest review. Your thoughts are valued and needed!

ALSO BY WHITNEY BAUSMAN

Herding Cats: The Chaotic, Exhausting & Hilarious Task of Parenting Toddlers

Toddlers are messy. Toddlers are moody. Toddlers have opinions and demands and emotions that flip from happy to hysterical in an instant. Essentially...**toddlers are cats**. And parenting them? Well, parenting toddlers is nonstop cat herding. 'Herding Cats' is an up-close, real-life look at the world of a toddler parent. A world of tantrums and potty training. A world of never-ending snot. A world of hilariously inappropriate comments, limitless growth, and perfectly timed "I love you's". From the author of 'Partly Sunny: An Honest and Humorous Look at the First Weeks of Bringing Home a Newborn' comes her toddler-filled follow-up. In this memoir bursting with laughter, commiseration, and encouragement, 'Herding Cats' empowers its readers to laugh off the toddler nonsense and find beauty in the midst of wrangling the most feral of felines.

ABOUT THE AUTHOR

Whitney Bausman lives in York, Pennsylvania with her husband and children. Whitney is a nurse by trade and studied health science and health education at the graduate level. At present, Whitney is a full-time mom to her toddlers. She fully believes that while life isn't always surface-level pretty, it *is* always big-picture beautiful.

Connect with Whitney:

Facebook fb.me/whitbaus
Instagram @prtlysunnyprnt
Twitter @prtlysunnyprnt

Made in the USA
Middletown, DE
26 May 2020